STUDIES IN MAJOR LITERARY AUTHORS

Edited by

William E. Cain
Professor of English
Wellesley College

T0386512

A ROUTLEDGE SERIES

STUDIES IN MAJOR LITERARY AUTHORS

WILLIAM E. CAIN, *General Editor*

COLONIALISM AND THE MODERNIST MOMENT IN THE EARLY NOVELS OF JEAN RHYS

Carol Dell'Amico

Routledge
Taylor & Francis Group

NEW YORK AND LONDON

From *Voyage in the Dark* by Jean Rhys. ©1968 by Jean Rhys. Used by permission of W.W. Norton & Company, Inc.

Excerpts from *Quartet* by Jean Rhys. ©1929, 1957 by Jean Rhys, used by permission of HarperCollins Publishers, Inc.

Excerpts from *After Leaving Mr. Mackenzie* by Jean Rhys, ©1931 by Jean Rhys, used by permission of HarperCollins, Inc.

From *Jean Rhys's Historical Imagination: Reading and Writing the Creole*, by Veronica Gregg. ©1995 by The University of North Carolina Press. Used by permission of the publisher.

Excerpts from "The Flaneur, the Sandwichman and the Whore: The Politics of Loitering," by Susan Buck-Morss, used by permission of the author.

Excerpts from *Coldness and Cruelty* by Gilles Deleuze, originally taken from *Venus in Furs* by Gilles Deleuze. ©1970 by Gilles Deleuze. Reproduced by permission of George Braziller, Inc.

Published in 2005 by
Routledge
Taylor & Francis Group
270 Madison Ave,
New York NY 10016

Published in Great Britain by
Routledge
Taylor & Francis Group
2 Park Square
Milton Park, Abingdon
Oxon OX14 4RN

© 2005 by Taylor & Francis Group, LLC
Routledge is an imprint of Taylor & Francis Group

Transferred to Digital Printing 2009

International Standard Book Number-10: 0-415-97528-X (Hardcover)
International Standard Book Number-13: 978-0-415-97528-5 (Hardcover)
Library of Congress Card Number 2005017532

Library of Congress Cataloging-in-Publication Data

Dell'Amico, Carol.
    Colonialism and the modernist moment in the early novels of Jean Rhys / by Carol Dell'Amico.
        p. cm. -- (Studies in major literary authors)
    Includes bibliographical references and index.
    ISBN 0-415-97528-X (acid-free paper)
    1. Rhys, Jean--Criticism and interpretation. 2. Modernism (Literature)--Caribbean Area. 3. Women and literature--Caribbean Area. 4. Modernism (Literature)--England. 5. Caribbean Area--In literature. 6. Imperialism in literature. 7. Colonies in literature. I. Title. II. Series: Studies in major literary authors (Unnumbered)

PR6035.H96Z634 2005
823'.912--dc22   2005017532

ISBN10: 0-415-97528-X (hbk)
ISBN10: 0-415-80341-1 (pbk)

ISBN13: 978-0-415-97528-5 (hbk)
ISBN13: 978-0-415-80341-0 (pbk)

Taylor & Francis Group
is the Academic Division of T&F Informa plc.

Visit the Taylor & Francis Web site at
http://www.taylorandfrancis.com

and the Routledge Web site at
http://www.routledge-ny.com

To my parents

Contents

Acknowledgments

Many people have contributed to this project. Thanks, first, to my dissertation committee at Rutgers University: Marjorie Howes, who I was so fortunate to have as a director, Bruce Robbins and John McClure. Many thanks also to my wonderful and always encouraging outside reader, Suzanne Chávez-Silverman. For unfailing support and enthusiasm, much hilarity, many ideas, and valuable feedback, I owe special debts of gratitude to Jane Phillips and Matthew Kaiser. Thanks also to Linda Schulze, Lisa Thompson, Wendy Silver, Weixing Su, Greg Chandler, Jonathan Ceniceros, Ken Urban, and my family, for so much love and such great friendship.

Abbreviations

ALMM   *After Leaving Mr. Mackenzie.* London and New York: W.W. Norton & Co., 1997.

GMM   *Good Morning, Midnight.* London and New York: W.W. Norton & Co., 1986.

Q   *Quartet.* London and New York: W.W. Norton & Co., 1997.

VD   *Voyage in the Dark.* London and New York: W.W. Norton & Co., 1982.

WSS   *Wide Sargasso Sea.* London and New York: W.W. Norton & Co., 1982.

Introduction

Jean Rhys's importance as a colonial voice within the postmodern is well established, thanks, largely, to *Wide Sargasso Sea* (1966). Her status as a colonial voice (if not a feminist one) within the modern, however, is less secure. This is mainly because her fictions have been distinguished as being either "Caribbean" or "European," and, since three out of the four modernist period novels have been deemed European, her peripheral status as a colonial commentator within Modernism seems quite evident.[1] That is, any colonial allusions and contexts of the European novels generally are considered incidental to the texts,[2] so that near contemporaries such as Conrad and contemporaries such as Joyce remain most prominent in postcolonial conversations about Modernism's literary coloniality.

This study revises this predominant perception of Rhys as only intermittently engaged with colonial questions within Modernism, asserting that she exercised a colonial specialty throughout the period. By illuminating highly developed colonial texts in each of the European novels and considering this colonial content alongside her Caribbean novel of the period, I demonstrate how each of these novels is shaped by the insights and concerns she developed as a displaced colonial and outsider for whom everything on her arrival to the foreign shore of the home country became strange.[3] In so doing, Rhys is revealed as a measured assessor of imperial modernist culture in one way through her method of employing of psychoanalytic tropes to refer to imperial formations. This is to say, the centrality of psychological and pathological symptomatics in Rhys's early texts points to the way in which she saw her writerly project within the modern as one of colonial "analysis."[4] More specifically, the readings here highlight Rhys's approach to selves, societies, and cultures as always "in process" within the context of the challenges and implications of emergent histories, groups, and conditions pursuant to the imperio-colonial events. Undoubtedly extrapolating from her experience and insights as one estranged, Rhys evinces a focus in her early fictions on the recognitions, transformations, and undoings the coming into consciousness of imperial history entails for Europe's subjects and cultures.

The overtly colonial *Voyage in the Dark* (1934), the subject of Chapter Two of this study, is the single novel of Rhys's modernist period set of four that so far has attracted sustained postcolonial attention. A first person narrative of a year in the life of a young Anglo/Welsh-Caribbean newly arrived to London, the novel is highly fragmentary. It is a montage of minute fragments—a collage of thoughts, events, and cultural allusions high and low—and the book's mass of fragments is organized into a montage yet again of events taking place either in the protagonist's London present, or else in her remembered (and mis-remembered) Caribbean past. To date, critics have argued that the novel's disposition of fragments conveys a critique of empire and the protagonist's identity crisis and split subjectivity. This chapter adds to that criticism by highlighting Rhys as a periodizer of the Euro-modernist moment through an examination of that which critics so far have skirted, namely the curious atmosphere of the novel, the effervescence, as it were, of protagonist Anna Morgan's way of being in London. I point to the motif of Anna's contagiousness in the novel, to how her breakdowns elicit the breakdowns of those around her, and to how the streets of London warp eerily about her, appearing to her to be haunted or to contain secrets. This gestating, haunted London and this contagious, disconcerting—colonial—protagonist I read alongside Homi K. Bhabha's writing on colonial unhomeliness and the unhomely (uncanny), in which the former is the strangeness following from "cross-cultural initiations" and the latter is a textual strategy that gestures toward unrepresented histories. Rhys's dis-eased and uneasy modernist London, in other words, is London periodized, a city where the fog of imperial repression is just beginning to lift.[5] Further, in an analysis of the related textual dynamics of the blocked alternations between London and the West Indies, I point to the way these geographic leaps are packaged as puzzles calling for solving, encouraging the recognition of obscured (repressed) global relations.

Rhys's critical examination of imperial culture and the European imperial subject begins, however, already in her first published novel, *Quartet* (1928), which is addressed in Chapter Four of this study. *Quartet*, most broadly, is a colonial allegory divided into two parts: a brief opening segment that sets up a problem and a main body detailing the course of a love affair that functions as a solution to the opening's problem. The novel's opening achieves its status as a problem calling for a response in two related ways.

First, it is an Enlightenment travesty, a piece of writing evoking revolutionary ideals against a history of compromise and ideals betrayed (Empire over Republic, the invention of racial hierarchies, the persistence of classism, and so on). Second, the opening sets up a rigorous allegorical opposition of the novel's two couples, its quartet of players: one couple is feminized, racialized, and underclassed as a unit, the other is masculinized, Europeanized, and so on. The novel, in short, is interested in the problem of exclusion, and imperial-era exclusion most specifically, since, in addition to class and gender, race and ethnicity are prominent preoccupations in the novel. That the novel's body—its story of a love affair—is a riposte to the opening's problems is gestured at through the way it constitutes a bridging of the opening's rigorously schematic oppositions: it involves one member of each couple, two lovers whose inexplicable attraction to their opposite number is a consequence of what Rhys constructs as their thoroughgoing abjection, in other words, their status as persons on fatally familiar terms with that which constitutes their identitarian undoing. This affair's elaboration of a radical dependence on "others," as I argue, conveys the particularities of a postcolonial ethics—the way in which one's others might come to be embraced.

That repression and abjection are primary, structuring formations within *Voyage in the Dark* and *Quartet* suggests, as I have said, the extent to which psychological tropes and dispositions serve Rhys in her exploration of problems in colonial history and culture. My reading of Rhys's second novel *After Leaving Mr. Mackenzie* (1931) in Chapter Three reinforces this understanding of her colonial literary method at the same time it demonstrates *Mackenzie*'s having been written after Conrad's colonial first novel *Almayer's Folly*. I argue that these two texts are written in the Masochian (masochistic) tradition as a means to critique imperial oppressions, an argument prefaced by my complication of the debate about masochism in Rhys in general. This debate concerns Rhys's apparent interest in depicting victim-like protagonists and the defeatism this evidently points to, and my complication ensues from the chapter's employment of a theory of masochism as yet unconsidered in the criticism. That is, following Gilles Deleuze's writing on the works of de Sade and von Sacher Masoch, I understand literary sadism and masochism's motifs and character types as formations referring to schemas of law and order. Thus, as Deleuze argues, whereas the novels of the revolutionary-era Sade refer to a perfected institutionalism where laws are no longer needed, the later Masoch was a minoritarian of a type, writing fervently against the consolidations of burgeoning state entities. Institutions of law and order to the masochist are not that which remain to be perfected, rather they are that which must always be constrained. Thus, as I say, both Rhys's and Conrad's masochistic protagonists (who are both morose dreamers and fantasists)—and the masochistic energies of the novels in general—are significant components of the texts' anti-imperial contents. Certainly, *Almayer's Folly* belongs with those of Conrad's (early anti-imperial) narratives depicting beset territories hosting any number of foreign presences destructively competing for trade and hegemony.[6] Rhys's prominent borrowing from *Almayer's Folly* in *After Leaving Mr Mackenzie*, which includes one lengthy excerpt from Conrad's text, revolves around her novel's central event of the decline and death of the protagonist's mother, a Brazilian Creole modeled after the Malay Mrs. Almayer. Following Conrad's novel, this event positions the daughter as the inheritor of what the text constructs as an unbearable imperial legacy.

For most critics, Rhys's final novel of the modernist period, *Good Morning, Midnight* (1939), is a quintessential (feminist) thirties novel. I build on this understanding of the novel in a first chapter by reading it for the first time in the criticism as a flaneur novel. Flaneur novels of Modernism such as Joyce's *Ulysses*, Woolf's *Mrs. Dalloway*, and Conrad's *The Secret Agent* are said to share an interest in exploring the nature of metropolitan life especially with respect to consumerism, although this estimation of the subgenre's particularity is evolving within postcolonial flaneur criticisms. Employing both earlier and later (postcolonial) flaneur criticisms, and building on the latter, I demonstrate that Rhys's novel is prominently concerned with consumerism and that this treatment of the market's power and breadth is projected, ultimately, on a global scale within an imperial historical context. Rhys filters her exploration of the market through the lens of thirties' fascism, tracing a global web of dehumanizing outcomes following from rationalizations rampant and unchecked: refugeeisms, racisms, and ghettoes of all stamps. This chapter also includes a brief analysis of *The Secret Agent* as a way of pointing to colonial affinities (again) between Rhys and Conrad's texts and to ways of viewing Anglophone flaneur novels' coloniality in general. In terms of this latter subject, I suggest that another way these novels constitute a subgenre is by virtue of the fact that all in some way ponder the problems of citizenship and/or identity within the context of imperio-globalism.

By the time Rhys was composing *Good Morning, Midnight*, her last published novel of the modernist period, she had not only lived in Europe far longer than she had ever lived in Dominica, she was also, as *Midnight* indicates, overcome with dread at the prospect of fascism and impending war. Yet, as we see, even as the novel evinces Rhys's profound preoccupation with the problems of the Europe in which she was living and writing, she is, at the same time, thinking globally. Indeed, to the extent that all of Rhys's major works of the modernist period yield compelling colonial content, it seems incumbent to acknowledge, finally, that there is an unbroken colonial continuum in Rhys's writing from the inception of her career to its end, and that the current line between the more overtly colonial texts and the rest is quite overdrawn.

Chapter One

Good Morning, Midnight: Flaneur Novels and the Colonial

Above the table on which a collection of cloth samples was unpacked and spread out—Samsa was a commercial traveler—hung the picture which he had recently cut out of an illustrated magazine and put into a pretty gilt frame. It showed a lady, with fur cap on and a fur stole, sitting upright and holding out to the spectator a huge fur muff into which the whole of her forearm had vanished!

—*Franz Kafka*, The Metamorphosis

To date, the feminist and anti-fascist polemics of *Good Morning, Midnight* have been most thoroughly explored in the criticism. Mary Lou Emery, for example, has explored how the book's treatment of male authority is developed as a problem of "fascistic authority" (171), invoking "the temptations of order and peace at any price" (145). Kate Holden, in a related vein, has more recently argued that the novel's preoccupation with "systems for identifying alleged insiders and outsiders" refers to "proto-fascist elements in English, bourgeois, patriarchal discourses and institutions" (144).

These readings by Holden and Emery, even as they stress Rhys's treatment of fascist complicity within Britain, dovetail with other recent readings. For example, Coral Ann Howells reads the novel as a "critique of male modernist representations" and treatment of women's "unbelonging" within Modernism (92), arguing that the novel demonstrates how "the woman writer [. . .] is effectively silenced [and] dispersed within a male-dominated literary space" (103). While Howells does not address the problem of fascism, her feminist reading nevertheless works well with Emery and Holden's idea that Rhys was writing under the threat of aggressively renewed masculinist ideologies and discourses. Veronica Marie Gregg's exploration of the novel's treatment of the special problems of cultural "outsiders" and "Others" coincides similarly with Emery and Holden's work, recalling, for instance, Holden's point that the novel traces an "unmappable territory" of outsiders "vulnerable to [. . .] the powerful monological voice of fascist ideology" (151).

My reading, here, will add to this body of criticism in a number of ways. First, I demonstrate that *Good Morning, Midnight* is a flaneur novel, i.e., a novel employing an urban pedestrian figure (flaneur) much like *Ulysses, Mrs. Dalloway,* and Conrad's *The Secret Agent.* Following Walter Benjamin's seminal writings on the literatures of "flanerie," most critics have explored the ways in which these texts' flaneurs indicate the works' concern at least in part with the nature of metropolitan culture and social life, and/or the urban culture and subjects of capital more particularly. Rhys's novel is paradigmatic in this regard, as character interactions in the novel are, as I demonstrate below, almost exclusively constructed as relations of "exchange." As such, the novel evinces Rhys's coincidence with contemporaneous anxieties over the burgeoning market and the societal changes this entails. This, then, points to how the novel's treatment of complicity and submission pertains not simply to fascism, but more broadly to the way in which any number of populaces were conferring on their leadership unprecedented legislative powers and the role of savior (i.e., no matter the particular ideologies and programs espoused). Thus, at the same time Rhys presents fascist currents as the most glaring indicator of generalized political submission in *Good Morning, Midnight,* she subsumes this development under the umbrella of a consolidating, aggressively interpellating, market in general. Indeed, as Holden points out, fascist ideology can be understood in the same terms as attendant programs of economic renewal, as both found their inspiration in the examples of American Fordism and Taylorism, i.e., in models of intensified rationalization and standardization.

However, beyond this, the broadest context within which the specter of a perniciously unchecked market is considered in *Good Morning, Midnight* is global, a component of the text which can be deemed its colonial dimension, and which, as I shall also argue, calls for a reconsideration of the significance of modernist period Anglophone flaneur novels in general. Postcolonial re-readings of Benjamin and of flaneur texts are, indeed, a growing field of flaneur criticisms. But, before turning to this recent scholarship, a review of the critical foundations of flaneur criticisms will be useful, both to illuminate the relationship to them of the more recent postcolonial speculations, and to prepare the ground for this chapter's exploration of *Good Morning, Midnight*'s discourse of "exchange."

Benjamin developed his theories of flaneur literatures primarily in writings on Charles Baudelaire, Paris of the nineteenth century, and various Surrealists, with his initial readers developing most extensively his ideas concerning the perceptive mode of flaneur text authors and/or characters. This mode, as they say, bespeaks a subjectivity in crisis, as metropolitan living and consumerism shape it. The distracted gazing of the flaneur-stroller is said to present experience as the apprehension of so many momentary, unconnected impressions and sensory shocks, so that in the flaneur's seduced, spectacle-consuming and mobilized gaze, as Susan Buck-Morss has written, "we recognize our own consumerist mode of being in the world" (*"Flaneur"* 105). Buck-Morss comments as follows on Benjamin's choice of "the flaneur, prostitute, [and] collector" as the "Ur-forms of contemporary life" (*"Flaneur"* 101):

> If the flaneur has disappeared as a specific figure, it is because the perceptive attitude which he embodied saturates modern existence, specifically, the society of mass consumption (and is the source of its illusions). The same can be argued for all of Benjamin's historical figures. In commodity society all of us are prostitutes, selling ourselves to strangers; all of us are collectors of things. (104)

The historical flaneur is a gentleman stroller whose "original habitat" was the Parisian arcades, "interior streets lined with luxury shops and open through iron and glass roofs to the stars" (103), and his disinterested viewing of spectacle (of passers-by and commodities for sale) has been, as Buck-Morss says, "preserved in the characteristic fungibility of people and things in mass society" (105).

In the opening to *Just Looking,* a book examining consumer culture in the fiction of Gissing, Dreiser, and Zola, Rachel Bowlby presents the changes in commercial activity in the mid-nineteenth century that gave rise to this commodified subjectivity:

> No longer do goods come to the buyers, as they had done with itinerant hawkers, country markets or small local stores. Instead, it is the buyers who have taken themselves to the product: and not, in this case, to buy, but more to "see" the things. In the 1960s, Guy Debord wrote forcefully of the *"spectacle de la marchandise,"* crystallizing the way that modern consumption is a matter not of basic items bought for definite needs, but of visual fascination and remarkable sights of things not found at home. People go out of their way [. . .] to look at displays of the marvels of

modern industrial production: there is nothing obviously functional in
a tourist trip. (1)

Since the flaneur commemorates and embodies these developments, this figure became for Benjamin a suitable icon with which to refer to every subject
under consumer-capitalism.

Turning now to postcolonial flaneur criticisms, the most common
point made in them tends to be that the metropolitan space of flaneur texts
refers to, as Rob Shields, for instance, has written, "elsewhere, to the colonized sites of production of the commodities on display, just as the colonial
hinterland is pervaded and transformed by codes which refer to the values
and domination of the metropolis" (68). According to Shields, this recognition occasions treatments of metropolitans in which both foreigners and
natives, or "outsiders and insiders," are equally "'dis-placed,'" as neither can
be said to be "properly at home in the commodified spaces of the imperial
metropolis" (68). Thus, more often than not, as Shields and others have suggested, a flaneur's pedestrianism is that of a subject whose observing gaze
becomes the means by which to regain mastery of the environment, "to par-
ticipate in the popular sense of empire, to master and even revel in the
'emporium'" (Shields 74).

Yet, there are arguments (including by Shields) that the genre points to
additional meanings. For instance, taking his cue from Benjamin's "fragmentary theory of the *flâneur* as the privileged personification of geographic dis-
location, cultural transgression, and conceptual reconfiguration," Rolf
Goebel proposes that "[i]n the *flâneur*'s subjectivity, instances of cultural and
historical hybridity acquire self-reflexive significance for the interpretation of
modernity" (378). This wilier, experimental flaneur is found elsewhere in flaneur (and other related) criticisms, in various guises. It is found in Édouard
Glissant's *Poetics of relation,* for example, in which migratory figures and literatures (texts of "errantry"), even those of Modernism, pose problems quite
apart from those of capitalist interpellation and imperial mastery. Beginning
with a consideration of the *Odyssey* and other related European, Icelandic and
African epics, Glissant explores the way in which so many migratory literary
figures indicate a text's desire, seemingly paradoxically, to conceive of a "root
identity." Glissant does not explain this seeming paradox in a way with which
we have lately become familiar, however, by proposing that all that is not
"home" in these texts serves only to highlight, in a phobic way, the desirabil-
ity of home and "the same" against all that is "other." Rather, he approaches
these texts' migrations and identitarian negotiations productively, arguing
that in texts of errantry a "root identity" is conceived of, crucially, through a

process of "enlightenment" in relation to cultural others, "through the Other" or "by taking up the problems of the Other," as he says (18). This other flaneur is found also in Rachel Bowlby's reading of Woolf's *"Street Haunting"* (1930), in which Woolf's street is a "place where [. . .] simple stereotypical distinctions" between groups "are broken down" (43), and in which flanerie indicates "transgressive" thought, that which "crosses and challenges set lines of demarcation, a step from a place represented as beyond the pale, out of bounds" (29). To these formulations we can add, as well, Kieran Keohane's characterization of Joyce's Bloom, whose mobility is a "permanent liminality," a "condition of coexistence with multiple Others, of mutually and self-reflexively negotiating the manifold encounters with alterity" (39).

This is not to say, however, that any of these latter writers would necessarily argue against the notion that the flaneur's mobility and mobilized gaze is indicative of homelessness or of the modern subject's captation by commodity spectacle; the point, rather, as I see it, is that any given flaneur text must be scrutinized for any number of negotiations. Further, what this means is that, at the same time any flaneur's mobility might indicate plight, the street in these texts might at the same time be functioning as the "privileged place of the performance of history" (Liston 1). In other words, the teeming metropolitan thoroughfare at any given moment in a flaneur text is the site of the individual's divestiture *or* the place where a salutary "collision" occurs between the individual and the "collective" (Liston 3). Indeed, as we see in Benjamin, the value of throwing oneself into public space—of the Dallowayan "plunge," as it were—is that one type of shock one might experience is an "awakening," allowing for a "critical deconstruction of the myths of modernity the city seeks to perpetuate" (Liston 6). Thus, in terms of these notions of reconnecting with the collective, of resuscitation, and of negotiations with alterities, those personages with whom textual flaneurs encounter in significant ways in these texts must be scrutinized. With whom, exactly, are an author's flaneur figures interacting in their perambulations? And why? To sum up, then, to the extent that a flaneur text might be exploring identity or its reconceptualization in terms of a cognizance of alterities *alongside* its consideration of intensifying market forces projected on a global scale or as imperial formations, the text might also include a consideration of the identitarian and other challenges following from the developing complexity of cross-cultural and geopolitical relations. This point becomes clear by a look at Conrad's *The Secret Agent,* an exercise that will, as well, provide useful points of comparison with my exploration of Rhys's novel.

The Secret Agent is a story about an *agent provocateur,* Verloc. Verloc has infiltrated the London anarchist and communist undergrounds and reports on their activities to his employer, a bureaucrat at the Russian Embassy. The novel begins with this Russian bureaucrat instructing Verloc to organize a bombing of a major London landmark, to the end of shocking the British authorities out of their complacent attitude as to the underground threat. He suggests the first meridian, the Greenwich Observatory, as target. Verloc is dismayed, knowing that this complacence is fully justified, but he capitulates to the plan in a bid to hang on to his job.

Verloc enlists the aid of his simple brother-in-law Stevie. When Stevie accidentally kills himself near the Observatory, the police are initially stumped, as they know, like Verloc, that the anarchist underground is dormant. Nevertheless, they learn quickly enough the true outlines of the case and set out to track down the malefactors (Verloc and his employer). The novel, however, ends inconclusively. As the Assistant Commissioner, the novel's detective, is closing in on Verloc, Mrs. Verloc, sister and caretaker of Stevie, kills her husband in a fit of sorrow and rage. The detective disappears from the novel because without Verloc he has nothing, and the novel's close follows Mrs. Verloc in her desperate attempt to flee London—which fails and culminates in her suicide.

Beyond this, there is the novel's principal flaneur, the detective in charge of the case, the Assistant Commissioner. A few suggestive details concerning this figure's curious profile, activities, and experiences—as well as the nature of Conrad's London—are worth compiling here. First, this figure is nameless, known only as the "Assistant Commissioner" throughout, and much, on many pages, is made of his appearance and personality in the novel. He is "dark," a "strange foreign fish," a "square peg in a round hole," a "thoughtful Don Quixote," and so on. The commissioner, furthermore, is an ex-colonial who hankers after his days in the "tropical colony," where, apparently, instituting control was a most satisfying matter, as societal divisions and standards of law and order were so clear-cut and artificial: "His career had begun in a tropical colony. He had liked his work there. It was police work. He had been very successful in tracking and breaking up certain nefarious secret societies amongst the natives" (78). He is, indeed, as Conrad puts it at one point, an Anglo-colonial situated at the center of "the Empire on which the sun never sets" (155). Yet, in London, by contrast, the commissioner is thoroughly frustrated with his work (that is, frustrated not simply with this case in particular). This frustration pertains to his lack of *grasp:* he is unable to get a clear fix on the metropolis he is supposed to be ordering, a plight compounded by the fact that his inferiors for various reasons keep him only nominally informed. His investigative forays into the streets and haunts of London, indeed, only intensify his sense of helplessness, his sense that he is unable satisfactorily to read and classify that which he encounters. Finding himself in an Italian restaurant in Soho, for example, he is said to make "to himself the observation that the patrons of the place had lost in the frequentation of fraudulent cookery all their national and private characteristics. And this was strange, since the Italian restaurant is such a peculiarly British institution" (111). In this restaurant, equally notable, albeit less ironic, the commissioner sees "himself in a piece of glass, and [is] struck by his foreign appearance," thereby "los[ing] more of his identity," an identity already eroded, presumably, by his earlier movements through the city. Conrad's London, in short, which is also the commissioner's, is "anarchic," opaque, no longer neatly classed, apparently no longer definitively British, mutable and mutating.

Considering these few suggestive details, it seems reasonable to say that Conrad's nameless, colonial, foreign-looking Assistant Commissioner is Shields's flaneur, a "'dis-placed,'" native-cum-foreigner figure serving Conrad to close "the gap between the (distant) foreign and the (local) intimate, violating the division of near and far and forcing us to rearrange our cognitive understanding of the spatial distribution of social relations" (68). Indeed, as Martin Ray has written, "the space of the city" in *The Secret Agent* is one of unsettling geographical "discontinuities," and, as such, Conrad's flaneur might encounter the shocking incongruity of a "rural idyll" upon emerging from a dark alley, and so forth. Further, as Ray says,

> the *political* geography of the city is just as subject to these ruptures and disjunctures, to the point where one can say that most of Chapter Two of *The Secret Agent* is set in imperial Russia. Verloc can turn off a London street and miraculously find himself in the territory of (what is presumably) Russia; as the Assistant Commissioner explains later to Vladimir [the Russian bureaucrat], "Embassies are supposed to be part and parcel of the country to which they belong." (206; emphasis added)

Considering the history of criticism of modernist texts, less recent explorations of Conrad's novel not surprisingly tend to emphasize the novel's apparent development of humans' isolation from one another, so that the attack on the Greenwich Observatory, the novel's most teasing, obviously symbolically loaded event, is seen as evidence of this theme of the impossibility of any shared apprehension of the world. Early critics' sense of Conrad's focus is, in my view, apt, if, in hindsight, too narrow. That is, what the "holes in space and time" (69) the blowing up of the Greenwich Observatory points to does indeed indicate Conrad's sense of the non-existence of a conceptually common world; however, taking into account Conrad's strange commissioner and recent flaneur criticisms, it is perhaps more apt to say that, for Conrad in this text, such a state of affairs follows from the fact of proliferating and increasingly complex global relations and exchanges. That is, no matter the (imperial) universalizing gesture the Washington Conference's establishment of universal time and space represents (Greenwich), undisputedly at issue post-Empire is the pressing problem of transnational, cross-cultural communication/translation and the related problem of geopolitical *opacity,* a crisis of geopolitical "cognitive mapping" (Jameson), as it were. Thus the novel's central problematics of identitylessness/multiculturalism (the commissioner's profile) and the fact that it is a *spy* novel about geopolitical lines of connection and influence *buried and hidden* (Britain's troubling susceptibility to foreign influence; the commissioner's troubling, persistent, lack of grasp). Indeed, as we see in Conrad's writing already by 1905, in essays such as *"Autocracy and War,"* the writer is pondering the fact that *"Il n'y a plus d'Europe*—there is only an armed and trading continent, the home of slowly maturing economical contests for life and death, and of loudly proclaimed world-wide ambitions" (*"Autocracy"* 112).[1] To this Conrad, we can connect Christopher GoGwilt's apt characterization of the author's evolving concerns, in which a movement is tracked from a focus on the impact of imperialism in colonial territories to an exploration of the changing map of Europe. This development Stephen Ross sees as one in which modernity becomes for Conrad that which Michael Hardt and Antonio Negri call "Empire," and which Ross describes as a "suppression of national interests by commercial interests in both the production of goods and services and the quest for markets and resources with which to continue the accelerating the cycle of production/consumption" (11). Thus, in terms of Conrad, Ross proposes that we should distinguish between those writings and textual formations concerned with the "imperialist world *in which* he wrote" versus "the incipiently Imperial world *about which*" he increasingly began writing (9; original emphasis).

In short, Conrad's flaneur in London is on one level an anxiously drawn global subject for whom exploding "holes in space and time" are the miasmic identitarian, geopolitical, and cross-cultural circumstances of, if not the day, then the days of "Empire" ahead. Hence, undoubtedly, in terms of *The Secret Agent,* Conrad's oft-noted refusal "to declare [any] political stance affirmatively, and the insistent undercutting of the various positions which emerge from it," and the fact that what "promises to be a detective story or a novel of espionage, a product of a genre founded on neat divisions of 'us' and 'them,' blows up the generic categories on which it is ostensibly founded"

(Erdinast-Vulcan 208, 215). In terms of this former point, it should be noted that, as Ian Watt has established, the Greenwich Park explosion of 14 February 1894 notwithstanding, *The Secret Agent,* like so many other of Conrad's novels, is only launched from historical events, which are then employed so as effectively disclaim "any relation to actual persons, places or events" (112). In other words, this is not a book whose central concerns are contemporaneous anarchist currents. Thus, further, in my view, in terms of this novel at least, the need to understand Conrad's elaboration of Russian influence beyond—or at least in addition to—his very real interest in the Russian influence on English political and literary culture so felt by Britons especially before WWI (Ash 2), beyond, even, the tragic fact that the early death of Conrad's parents followed from their imprisonment by the Russian authorities for their (or mainly his father's) activities in Poland against Russian imperialism. Rather, again, these events, feelings, and circumstances are harnessed by Conrad to the end of elaborating the idea of the disorienting complexity and opacity of metropolitan and transnational relations—which is to say that *The Secret Agent* is, indeed, a novel of "Empire."

Rhys's text, as I shall demonstrate, is a novel of Empire as well, although the notion of the fragility of national identities in particular is a more decided focus, one which perhaps follows from what is, reasonably, considering *Good Morning, Midnight*'s publication date of 1939, its far greater focus on market determinations.[2] Indeed, these novels' differing focuses are attested to in the particular central symbol each author chooses to anchor his/her text's explorations. In Conrad's novel, we are proffered the spectacle of the ruin of universal space and time, and in Rhys's we are presented with the "Exhibition," an international exhibition erected in the Paris in which the novel takes place and which fascinates Rhys's protagonist during her Parisian sojourn. This exhibition, like Conrad's bombing, refers to a real event given the dating of the novel's action, the 1937 *Exhibition Internationale des Arts et des Techniques Appliqués à la Vie Moderne.* Rhys declines to name the exhibition in question, however, a reticence undoubtedly designed to connote altogether Europe's succession of great exhibitions, i.e., those of England and France (and, subsequently, of the United States). These are the exhibitions that, after the mid-nineteenth century, "took on the function of imperial display, ordering and presenting the human and material resources of empire to metropolitan audiences" (Hinsley 120). *Good Morning, Midnight*'s exhibition, as I will demonstrate, is synonymous in the novel with the global reach of imperio-capital, a scenario Rhys filters through the fascist 1930s, projecting a rationalizing world beset by proliferating racisms, (labor and other) ghettoes, and forced migrations of all kinds. Thus, whereas geopolitical and geocultural communicative and cognitive concerns most thoroughly preoccupy the anxious Conrad, Rhys's primary concern in her flaneur novel of Empire is more narrowly that of automatization, the dehumanization that follows from rationalizations run amok. But, first, before tracing the particular, global map of *Good Morning, Midnight,* I present the novel's elaboration of the triumph of "exchange."

EXCHANGE

Sasha Jensen of *Good Morning, Midnight* is a flaneur. She is, for the duration of the novel, a tourist of sorts, because she is on a two-week holiday to Paris from London, and her plan for her vacation is simply to eat and to walk and to do a little shopping (the novel begins just as she has checked into her hotel in Paris and ends a day or two before she leaves). She is not quite a full-fledged tourist, however, because she once lived in Paris and so the city is also in some sense a home. Indeed, pertinent to the story is that Sasha conceives of her vacation plan—her strict plan only to consume (eat, drink, shop, sight-see)—as a way to preclude any remembering of her past. That is, she sets out for the holiday with the specific, resolute intention of being no more and no less than a perfect tourist. But, despite these well-laid plans, she is not in Paris for very long before she must give up trying not to remember, as landmarks and familiar places spark a flood of memories that cannot be capped. The novel's key conceptual oppositions of tourist/native (homeless/home) and forgetting/memory thus point to Sasha's paradigmatic drama of flanerie, and to how her pedestrianism figures as both plight and solution, as both diagnosis and antidote. At the same it indicates her status as an urban automaton, she will enjoy over the course of her vacation a salutary resuscitation of self pursuant to her Dallowayan "plunge" into public space. Sasha, in other words, must take on the difficulty of constructing a self amidst a whirlwind of urban traffic and spectacle, foregoing her pursuit of numbness.

Good Morning, Midnight's dialogue with precursor flaneur literatures is scrupulous: Sasha within the introductory pages is presented as a prototypical window-shopping flaneur, and the novel thereafter sounds one flaneur trope after another. I begin with the passage in which Sasha is this window-shopper, recalling how it is she came to be in Paris in the first place:

> I had just come from my little health-stroll round Mecklenburgh Square and along the Gray's Inn Road. I had looked at this, I had looked at that, I had looked at the people passing in the street and at a shop-window full

of artificial limbs. I came in to somebody [Sidonie, a friend] who said: 'I
can't bear to see you looking like this.'
   'Like what?' I said.
   'I think you need a change. Why don't you go back to Paris for a bit?
. . . You could get yourself some new clothes [. . .]. (11)

Sasha's walking in the above is an exercise in desultory looking "at this" and
"at that," at faceless, nameless people "passing" by. This is a world in which
humans are commodified to the bone, commodified, that is, to the extent
that they can be imagined as so many "artificial limbs," the novel's first but
by no means last image of a mechanized humanity. Sasha, certainly, is intent
on remaining numb before she gives into remembering, believing, evidently,
that dredging up a painful past will not "re-member" her at all but rather tear
her apart all over again:

> The thing is to have a programme, not to leave anything to chance—no
> gaps. No trailing around aimlessly with cheap gramophone records
> starting up in your head, no 'Here this happened, here that happened.'
> Above all, no crying in public, no crying at all if I can help it. (15)

No painful retro-spection and no making a spectacle of herself are, then, the
"programme," and memory is likely to be colonized before the fact by
"cheap," standardized, mass-produced versions of experience anyway.[3]
   Yet, Sasha does not live up to her prescribed "programme." She ends up
making a spectacle of herself on more than one occasion and she also gives
into remembering fairly soon:

> I walk along, remembering this, remembering that, trying to find a
> cheap place to eat—not so easy around here. The gramophone record is
> going strong in my head: 'Here this happened, here that happened. . . .'
>   I used to work in that shop just off this street.
>   I can see myself coming out of the Métro station at the Rond-Point
> every morning at half-past eight, walking along the Avenue Marigny,
> turning to the left and then to the right, putting my coat and hat into
> the cloak-room, going along a passage and starting in with: 'Good
> morning, madame. Has madame a vendeuse?' (17)

Immediately following this passage, the first long sequence of remembering
in the novel begins. Sasha first recalls her job as a dress house hostess, then a
whole sequence of past jobs:

Thinking of my jobs. . . .
There was that one I had in the shop called Young Britain [. . . .] Little
boys' sailor suits were there, and young gentlemen's Norfolk suits were
there. . . . Well, I got the sack from that in a week, and very pleased I
was too.
Then there was that other job—as a guide. (30)

Sasha doesn't last long at Young Britain, and she doesn't last long as a tourist
guide for "American Express" either (31). Yet, she has a bit more to remember in the text about her job as a guide. What she remembers is her first
client, a female tourist for whom the passing of fashion is the be all and end
all of existence:

> Now she wants to be taken to the exhibition of Loie Fuller materials
> and she wants be taken to the place where they sell that German camera
> which can't be got anywhere else outside Germany, and she wants to be
> taken to a place where she can buy a hat which will épater everybody
> she knows yet be easy to wear, and on top of all this she wants to be
> taken to a certain exhibition of pictures. (31)

In this scenario, hats "épater" better than even art, and art is every modernist's nightmare: a matter of passing fashion, "characteristically fungible,"
no different than a hat, one commodity amongst others. We realize also in
reading this passage that, since Sasha has come to Paris in order to buy herself a new set of clothes ("You could get yourself some new clothes"), and
since she is only a visitor, despite her history there, she has moved from being
a tourist guide and salesperson to being a tourist and shopper. Now she will
not ask, but rather be asked, "'Good morning, madame. Has madame a
vendeuse?'" So, although Sasha is in some sense home, she is initially characterized, nonetheless, so that we understand she has donned the identities of
the women whom she served in her earlier life (and the first item of clothing
she buys, even, is a hat).

Sasha, then, appears in many ways to be no different from the exhibi-
tion-mad woman above. Yet, as we see, her manner of being this woman is
often rendered as a deliberate and ironic form of impersonation: "I must go
and buy a hat this afternoon, I think, and tomorrow a dress. I must get on
with the transformation act" (63). Or, at one point in the novel, she quite lit-
erally pretends to be the hat women of yore to two men she has met on the
street and with whom she is having a drink: "I tell them [. . .] that I am over
here for two weeks to buy a lot of clothes to startle my friends—my many

friends" (47). Further underscoring Sasha's non-coincidence with women she served in her earlier life is that, while she buys some pieces of clothing, she can't afford to buy so very many, and, further, we know that she has had to borrow money for the trip from Sidonie. We know, also, that she has few friends. Thus she is not quite, after all, the obviously wealthy female tourist of the past—but, then again, Sasha is not poverty stricken as she was in her earlier life. She has in the meantime come into a small inheritance:

> I shall receive a solicitor's letter every Tuesday containing £2 10s od. A legacy, the capital not be touched. . . . 'Who?' . . . When I heard I was very surprised—I shouldn't have thought she liked me at all. 'You may consider yourself very fortunate,' he said, and when I saw the expression in his eyes I knew exactly why she did it. She did it to annoy the rest of the family. . . . (42)

So, once poor and struggling and not succeeding in keeping her head above water, Sasha was, as she says to herself on more than one occasion, "Saved, rescued, fished-up, half-drowned" (10). Then again, money enough she may have now, but in her mind she is permanently damaged goods: "(Saved, rescued, but not quite so good as new. . . .)" (93).

Further impeding a grasp of Sasha's precise status in the novel is this ambiguous passage in which Sasha is constructed as semi-wealthy, semi-successful, a semi-tourist and so forth once again:

> Now, what are they [hotel *patron,* chambermaid, and potential guest] saying? 'Marthe, montrez le numéro douze.' And the price? Four hundred francs a month. I am paying three times as much as that for my room on the fourth floor. It shows that I have ended as a successful woman, anyway, however I may have started. One look at me and the prices go up. And when the Exhibition is pulled down and the tourists have departed where shall I be? In the other room, of course—the one off the Gray's Inn Road, as usual trying to drink myself to death. . . . (34)

Here, Sasha seems to distinguish herself from the common run of tourist who is in Paris for the exhibition. She seems amused that hoteliers take her for a typical tourist with money to burn. In the same breath, however, she seems momentarily to be taken by others' perception of her and to adopt their point of view. She thinks that she is, indeed, a "successful woman." Yet, the passage ends with an image that belies this. Strip away her seductive packaging and her truth is found: she is a woman who spends her days trying to drink herself "to death."

Sasha both is and is not the fashion house shoppers and the female tourist of a decade past. To the extent that she is, though, Rhys has advanced the following proposition: There are no relations between people or people and things beyond those determined by consumption and the market; one is, at any given moment, either a buyer or seller, a guide or sight-seer, and so on. To the extent that Sasha follows and mimics the female tourist and shoppers of the past, then, both her thorough imbrication within and her complicity with the status quo is suggested. The ambiguity of her persona, however, remains, and it suggests a more complex problem whose nature, I believe, is illuminated by her interactions with the novel's small host of minor characters.

Sasha spends her days in Paris walking from restaurant to bar, catching sight of familiar landmarks and so being thrown into memory. Her remembrances take up a good portion of the novel, roughly half of it, so that by the novel's end we are privy to a reasonably coherent history of Sasha's entire adult life. Beyond this, however, are Sasha's meetings with various men, the novel's secondary characters. The first two characters are Russians who approach her one day in the street, perceiving, they say, that she is sad. They invite her to a drink. One of them, a "naturalized Frenchman" by the name of Nicolas Delmar, makes a date to meet with her again as he wishes to introduce to her a friend of his, another Russian, the artist Serge Rubin (64). Besides her encounters with these Russians, Sasha meets a few times with a young, male prostitute, René, who approaches her one evening when she is leaving a café. And, finally, there is the nameless man (whose name she never learns) who has the room next to hers at the hotel. Even though she appears to dislike this man on first sight, it becomes clear that there is, in fact, an understanding between them.

The passage from the novel excerpted just above about Sasha's impressive appearance pertains to these encounters she has with these various men. It does so because in the case of the Russians and René, they appear to be interested in her for her show of relative wealth. Or, more precisely, Sasha is certain that everybody who thinks she is wealthy—the Russians, René, and the patron of the hotel included—is taken in by her fur coat, a gift she would sell if this did not mean offending its giver (184): "Just then two men [Delmar and the other Russian, but not Serge] come up from behind and walk along either side of me. One of them says: 'Pourquoi êtes-vous si triste?'" (45). Sasha, so sinisterly surrounded and familiarly addressed in this way (a "female version of flanerie," as Buck-Morss observes, is "[p]rostitution") opts first for silence but then decides to speak (*"Flaneur"* 119). She has just thought that, yes, she is as miserable as a sorry circus-spectacle: "Yes, I am sad, sad as a circus-lioness" (45). But when she speaks, she lies instead: "'But I'm not sad. Why should you think I'm sad?'" (45).

After some preliminaries, the three make their way to a bar where Sasha continues to dissemble, pretending, as I have already said, that she is the breezy female tourist she once served as guide:

> The usual conversation. . . . I say that I am not sad. I tell them that I am very happy, very comfortable, quite rich enough, and that I am over here for two weeks to buy a lot of clothes to startle my friends—my many friends. The shorter man, who it seems is a doctor, is willing to believe that I am happy but not that I am rich. He has often noticed, he says, that Englishwomen have melancholy expressions. It doesn't mean anything. The other one [Nicolas] is impressed by my fur coat, I can see. He is willing to believe that I am rich but he says again that he does- n't think I am happy. (47)

Whether or not Delmar is deceived, and whether or not this matters, is not clear at this point in the novel. Still, he asks her to meet with him again, this next time, as I have said, so that he might introduce her to Serge. Sasha agrees to the plan but on second thoughts does not make the appointment. Yet, on the day after they were supposed to meet, Delmar catches sight of her on the street once again, begs her to follow through, and so she finally ends up meeting Serge. In the meantime, Delmar succeeds in getting Sasha to admit that she is not happy. He claims that friends are easy to make and the key to contentment, and he will prove all this to Sasha by introducing her to his: "'But I have many friends. I'll introduce you to all of them if you wish. Will you allow me? Then you will never be alone and you'll be much happier, you'll see'" (67).

The third meeting with Delmar eventually occurs and the two make their way to Serge's studio. All seems to be going well until Sasha dissolves into tears, overcome, apparently, by Delmar and Serge's sincere demonstra- tion of friendship. This is the third time in the novel Sasha violates her pledge not to make a spectacle of herself. However, whereas in the first and second instances her tearful displays are met with frigid disapproval, "'I understand. All the same. . . . Sometimes I'm just as unhappy as you are. But that's not to say that I let everybody see it'" (10), in this case they are met with compassion: "'Oh, madame, oh, madame,' Delmar says, 'why do you cry?'", and with crisp matter-of-factness: "'But cry,' le peintre says. 'Cry if you want to. Why shouldn't you cry? You're with friends'" (93). The after- noon is not ruined after all, and the three go on to discuss a number of things, including tears: "We seriously discuss the subject of weeping" (94).

Although Sasha's weeping does not put a damper on proceedings, there occurs what the reader understands is a real crisis. It turns out that Nicolas and Serge, all along, have been planning to ask Sasha to buy one of Serge's paintings. This development is a problem because, by now in the course of events, her association with these men has evolved into a kind of test in relation to the proposition early on advanced in the novel. Instead of the notion that there is no escaping the all-encompassing net of the market, a running question has taken its place, thanks to Delmar and despite Sasha's early suspicions of his motivations: Are there relations beyond those shaped by the rule of commodity exchange? Has Sasha met someone who is truly interested in her well-being and who has no ulterior motives? Is not Delmar insisting that he is a friend and has not Serge taken up the refrain himself ("You're among friends")?

Serge announces that he must leave for an appointment:

> A dialogue with Delmar as to the best way to get to this place, which seems to be in the Rue du Bac. He turns at the door and, with the mocking expression very apparent, says something in Russian. At least, I suppose it's Russian.
>
> [. . . .]
> 'What did he say before he went out?'
> 'He said that if you didn't want to buy a picture you needn't buy one. Nobody expects you to.' (98–9)

Delmar's words suggest that it has been understood all along that Sasha is visiting Serge for the purpose of purchasing a "picture," but this is not the case. Sasha, however, displays neither surprise nor a sense of betrayal, and she does not appear to feel that her loneliness has been exploited by Delmar: "'Oh, but I do. I absolutely want one.'" (99). Delmar puts up an exhibition of Serge's paintings for Sasha's private viewing: "There are a lot of empty frames stacked up against the wall. Delmar arranged them round the room and put the canvases one by one in them" (99). When Sasha chooses a painting of an "old Jew" "playing the banjo" (100), Serge returns, and they discuss the price:

> 'The price of that is six hundred francs,' he says. 'If you think it's too much we'll arrange some other price.'
>
> All his charm and ease of manner have gone. He looks anxious and surly. I say awkwardly: 'I don't think it at all too much. But I haven't got the money. . . .'

Before I can get any further he bursts into a shout of laughter. 'What did I tell you?' he says to Delmar.

'But have it, take it, all the same. I like you. I'll give it you as a present.'

'No, no. All I meant was that I can't pay you now.'

'Oh, that's all right. You can send the money from London. I'll tell you what you can do for me—you can find some other idiots who'll buy my pictures.'

When he says this, he smiles at me so gently, so disarmingly. The touch of the human hand. . . . I'd forgotten what it was like, the touch of the human hand.

'I'm serious. I mean that. Take the picture and send me the money when you can.'

'I can let you have it tonight.'

We argue for some time as to where we shall meet. (100–1)

The immediate significance of this episode and of Serge's surliness seems fairly clear. Serge is embittered over his need to engage in the business of selling art, and Sasha must decide to trust that these men are sincere in their offers of friendship despite their need of her money and patronage.

This much about Serge, certainly, we glean from Delmar's isolated confidences about him. Serge once mounted a very successful exhibition of his works, but he had to be cajoled into doing so and since then he has refused to do so again:

'Le peintre,' he says, 'he's mad. [. . . .] However, I talked to him and in the end he managed to get the money to give his exhibition. And his pictures were bought. Yes, they were bought. . . . Eighteen thousand francs. [. . . .] All the same he is mad.' (102–3)

Serge's madness is his refusal to play the art-as-business game, and, possibly, his preference for customers such as Sasha, purchasers with whom he feels he has some connection other than purely business ones.

More broadly, however, this episode sheds light on Rhys's ambiguous rendering of Sasha's status. Sasha is both weak and strong, at any moment successful or damaged, because in coming up in the world she has not moved from being someone who was exploited to somebody potentially able to exploit. She is positioned as a buyer in this scenario (indeed, once again, she is likened to the female tourist because she is at an exhibition of sorts), but she is, nevertheless, quite possibly, subject to exploitation. That is, there is the possibility that Delmar and Serge have been so kind only so as to more effectively fleece her. In other words, Sasha may have the money here, but Delmar has the manipulative means to extract it from her. Yet, if Delmar is manipulating Sasha, he might be doing so only in an effort to help his beloved friend. Or, Serge himself might be manipulating Sasha, but if so, he does so only because he cannot escape the exigencies of the burgeoning market.

Thus, insofar as Sasha's relations with the Russians take the form of a test in the novel (are there relations untainted by the rule of commodity exchange?), Rhys's answer suggests a provisional no. While on the one hand we glimpse the communion of Delmar and Serge and the larger, Russian, expatriate (semi-) community to which they belong, on the other we sense that their solidarity rests, precisely, on their mutual need to engage with the market (they appear to function as a team of sorts: Delmar seeks out likely customers and conveys them to Serge). Or, although we tentatively trust in Delmar and Serge's sincere concern for Sasha, she would not have been brought into their circle in the first place if it were not for her presumed purchasing power (the class marker of the fur coat). Indeed, as Judith Kegan Gardiner so aptly says, *Good Morning, Midnight*'s titular citation from the Emily Dickinson poem points to the novel's demonstration that "apparent oppositions collapse when brought into close juxtaposition" (234). Everyone in Rhys's flaneur novel is at once seducing and seduced, exploiting and exploited: everybody, first and foremost, is subject to the rule of the market.

That the novel does, indeed, take the form of a running question and series of tests is confirmed by Sasha's relationship with René, the "gigolo." Her encounters with René stretch, as do her meetings with the Russians, through the course of the novel, and they mirror her experiences with Delmar and Serge in a number of explicit ways. As in the case of Delmar, we are led to believe that Sasha's fine fur coat takes in René, who, as I have said, first approaches her one evening when she is leaving a café. By now, she not only has her new hat in addition to her fur, but, as well, a wonderful new coiffure ("'In your place, madame, I shouldn't hesitate. But not for moment. A nice blond cendré'" [61]):

> As we walk along, I look sideways at him and can't make him out. He isn't trying to size me up, as they usually do—he is exhibiting himself, his own person. He is very good-looking, I noticed that in the Dôme. But the nervousness, the slightly affected laugh. . . .
>
> Of course. I've got it. Oh Lord, is that what I look like? Do I really look like a wealthy dame trotting round Montparnasse in the hope of—? After all the trouble I've gone to, is that what I look like? I suppose I do. (72)

With this, Sasha the flaneur and (art) collector meets a prostitute, and so all of Benjamin's "[u]r-forms of contemporary life" are, in a precise correspondence, circulating within Rhys's novel. With the above, also, Rhys again sounds the novel's central trope of exhibition/ism. Further, we see again Sasha's conviction that she doesn't quite fit into her skin, that there is a discrepancy between who she is and how she appears to others.

Sasha's interactions with René point to a blurring and complication of distinctions, just as her relations with the Russians do. But this time they do so with a bit of a difference: "He is looking straight ahead, gathering himself up for some effort. He is going to say his piece. I have done this so often myself that it is amusing to watch somebody else doing it" (73). Just as Sasha has moved from being tour guide to tourist and from salesperson to buyer, so now she is positioned as the seduced rather than the seducer.

Yet, even as René makes a valiant effort to sell himself as she once used to do, Sasha is not at all convinced that all of the power in their relation lies with her. In response to her challenging question, "'Why do you want to talk to me?'", René's rejoinder disconcerts her:

> He says: 'Because I think you won't betray me.'
> [. . . .]
> Of course I won't betray you. Why should I betray you?'
> 'No,' he says, 'Why?'
> He throws his head back and laughs. That's the gesture of showing
> off the teeth. Also, I suppose he is laughing at the idea of my being able
> to betray him. (73)

Sasha's thoughts point to how René is invested with powers pursuant to generational and gender power dynamics that are not wholly voided by their differing economic statuses. Prostitute and so "seller and commodity in one" he might be, as Buck-Morss might put it, but Sasha, as Gardiner points out, must struggle with "the destructive polarization of older woman and sexual woman" (244). René, clearly, is desperately in need of immediate funds, and it is quite possible that he, like Delmar and Serge before him, perceives Sasha's loneliness and sees her as an easy touch.

The story of Sasha and René, too, evolves into a test. While Sasha is able to shake off René this first night, she is not successful in banishing him once and for all. Opening her door to a knock a day or two later, she finds him standing outside. Since René proves resistant to both reason and insult and cannot be repelled, she gives in to allowing him to tag along on an outing or two. And, soon enough, she begins to wish that René is sticking to her not because he thinks he can finally overcome her defenses, but because he is interested in her company.

Sasha and René's association ends on what appears to be Sasha's last or near-to-last night in Paris. They have said their (last) goodbyes, but, as Sasha is unlocking the door to her room, she finds that René has not in fact wandered off but rather has clandestinely followed her upstairs. He embraces her and her defenses crumble; but their attempt at lovemaking is a disaster. Sasha, finally, cannot believe that René is making love to her for any other reason than his need of money. Miserably, huddled on the bed with her eyes shaded, she tells him to leave with the "thousand-franc" note that is in a dressing-case on the room's table, and to leave the other notes in the case, so she can pay her hotel bill. Once he has left she checks to see what he has taken, believing he will have made off with every last *centime,* the money for her hotel bill included. But, in fact, although she has heard him walk over to the table and stop there, it turns out that he has taken nothing at all. "Here's to you, gigolo," she thinks (186).

Sasha's hotel, Rhys tells us at the novel's start, is situated in a cul-de-sac, "What they call an impasse" (9). This is the novel's opening:

> 'Quite like old times,' the room says. 'Yes? No?'
>
> There are two beds, a big one for madame and a smaller one on the opposite side for monsieur. The wash-basin is shut off by a curtain. It is a large room, the smell of cheap hotels faint, almost imperceptible. The street outside is narrow, cobble-stoned, going sharply uphill and ending in a flight of steps. What they call an impasse. (9)

Much of *Good Morning, Midnight* takes place in between this Yes and this No, balanced precariously on this conceptual impasse. On the one hand, times have changed for Sasha because she no longer seduces men for patronage and neither is she obliged to suffer menial employment and so abase herself before employers. Moreover, her relatively secure financial position substantially transforms power dynamics between her and others, especially men. On the other hand, while men now pursue her for money as opposed to her person, her relations with them are still thoroughly tinctured by power dynamics pursuant to the (same old) institutionalized sex-gender inequalities. And, further and finally, while Sasha's money empowers her to a certain degree, this only means, within the terms of the novel, that her relative position within a network of exchange *that hasn't changed,* has changed.

THE GLOBAL EXHIBITION

The secure, all-encompassing network of market exchange figures in the novel as the Exhibition. Indeed, whereas Sasha seems to distinguish herself from the common run of tourist at one point in the novel, while she seems to suggest, that is, that she herself is not in Paris for the exhibition ("And when the Exhibition is pulled own and the tourists have departed where shall I be?"), in fact, near the novel's end, we find that she has been visiting it all along:

> 'I'm going to the Exhibition,' I say. 'I want to see it again at night before I go.'
> 'The Exhibition?' [this is René]
> 'Haven't you been to it?'
> 'No, I haven't.' 'What should I do at the Exhibition?'
> 'Well, I'm going. You needn't come if you don't want to. I'll go by myself.'
> I want to go by myself, to get into a taxi and drive along the street, to stand by myself and look down at the fountains in the cold light.
> 'But of course,' he says. 'If you want to go to the Exhibition, we'll go. Naturally.' (163)

Mary Lou Emery describes the 1937 *Exhibition Internationale des Arts et des Techniques Appliqués à la Vie Moderne* as follows:

> The novel opens and closes with significant allusions to the exhibition, allusions which set the novel firmly within a Paris of intense social and political conflict, symbolized best perhaps by the two major buildings of the exposition which confronted one another directly on each side of the Champs de Mars—that of the Soviet Union, topped by giant figures of a marching man and woman with hammer and sickle held high, and that of Nazi Germany, crowned by an immense gold eagle grasping a swastika in its claws. (144)

Close to the novel's beginning, apparently on her first night in Paris, Sasha dreams:

> I am in the passage of a tube station in London. Many people are in front of me; many people are behind me. Everywhere there are placards printed in red letters: This Way to the Exhibition, This Way to the

> Exhibition. But I don't want to go to the Exhibition—I want the way
> out. There are passages to the right and passages to the left, but no exit
> sign. Everywhere the fingers point and the placards read: This Way to
> the Exhibition. . . . I touch the shoulder of the man walking in front of
> me. I say: 'I want the way out.' But he points to the placards and his
> hand is made of steel. I walk along with my head bent, very ashamed,
> thinking: 'Just like me—always wanting to be different from other peo-
> ple.' The steel finger points along a long stone passage. This Way—This
> Way—This Way to the Exhibition. . . . (13)

Sasha's refusal of both "left" and "right" points to a rejection of both the
Soviet and fascist solutions to Europe's predicament, and her sense of there
being "no exit" points to the novel's broadest concern and conviction: the
Exhibition is what remains and is that from which, ultimately, there will be
no escape: "This Way to the Exhibition, This Way to the Exhibition [. . . .]
This Way to the Exhibition. . . . [. . . .] This Way—This Way—This Way to
the Exhibition. . . ." (13). Thus, whereas a tempering socialism presented
itself to Rhys's contemporaries even after the worst of the recession was over
as the only acceptable and indeed viable long term solution to Europe's problems, Rhys's vision, clearly, is hardly sanguine.

That the heavy impress of the market is developed in *Good Morning,
Midnight* most broadly as an imperio-global problematic, in which, further,
the novel's critique of fascism is subsumed under a larger polemic concerning the perniciousness of unchecked rationalizations in general, can be
demonstrated in a number of ways. A look at the novel's embedded story of
a Martiniquean mulatto, for example, is illustrative in this regard. Serge tells
the story of the Martiniquean the day Sasha visits his studio; he and the
Martiniquean were living in the same rooming-house when he was living in
London. He says that he came home one day to find her lying in a passage
of the hotel crying, experiencing a breakdown, overcome, finally, by her
racist treatment at the hands of Londoners in general and the other roomers
in particular. To date in the criticism, Kate Holden has addressed this inter-
lude most substantively, in her exploration of how such works as *Good
Morning, Midnight,* Kate Burdekin's *Swastika Nights,* and various writings
by Woolf all propose that "proto-fascist" formations were "endemic" in
English institutions (144). Holden, aptly, considers Serge's story in light of
Sasha's "empathetic choice" of the painting of the Jewish street musician,
Rhys's strategy of having a Jewish character relate a story of persecution, and
Sasha's thinking of being cruel as becoming "devastatingly English" in char-
acter. That is, in terms of this last point, while establishing that Sasha, René,

Serge and Delmar are a group of social outcasts "vulnerable to [. . .] the monological voice of fascist ideology" (151), Holden makes the further point that Rhys wishes us to understand that even these outsiders, including Sasha herself, are susceptible to the powerful fascist allure:

> Rhys makes it clear that, from [Sasha's] first meeting with René, Sasha has fantasies of humiliating him: 'I had meant to get this man to talk to me and tell me all about it, and then be so devastatingly English that perhaps I should manage to hurt him a little in return for all the many times I've been hurt.' Torturers and victims can be interchangeable, but the specific historical context should not be overlooked. (152)

The critic sums up her gloss on Rhys's text as follows:

> Indeed, in defining the sadistic impulse as 'devastatingly English,' Rhys proposes that the English have a special facility in this regard, a mechanics of superiority/inferiority, of domination/subordination born, as Woolf's writing also insists, of the history of Imperialism, colonialism, and the arrogant confidence of bourgeois men. (153)

As Holden asserts, in linking the persecuted, dehumanized mulatto woman to the Jewish Serge, Rhys points to institutional fascism at home by drawing a connection between fascism and imperialism on the basis of their shared mechanics of "superiority/inferiority." Yet, what a further consideration of this portion of the novel illuminates is that Rhys's linking of the two cultures, in this regard, is quite explicitly presented as a problematic following from a mutually informing market dynamic of exploitative labor rationalizations. Thus, when Sasha arrives to Serge's studio, what she sees, first, is a number of West African masks ranged along the walls:

> 'West African masks?'
> 'Yes, straight from the Congo. . . . I made them. This one isn't bad.' (91)

No sooner than Serge admits to capitalizing on the contemporaneous fad for African artifacts, we find the painter putting "on some beguine music, Martinique music, on an old gramophone in the corner" (92). Having transported the reader from (an ersatz) Africa to the West Indies in this way, Rhys next conveys the reader from the Caribbean to the Paris of the story, in the form of a desultory consideration of which Caribbean-themed "boîtes" in Paris are in fashion and which out:

Then we talk about Negro music and about various boîtes in Montparnasse. The Highball? No, the Highball isn't nice any more. It's a dirty place now. Oh, is it? Yes, it is. Nobody goes there now. But the Cuban Cabin in Montmartre, that's quite good. You might like that. They play very well there. It's gay. (93)

Since Rhys presents Serge's story of the mulatto woman immediately after this particular series of African/Caribbean allusions, these additional elements must inform our understanding of Serge's story about the Martiniquean and these characters' combined significance. And, as we see, this tracing of the imperial byways of commodities and this notion of an easy commodification of cultures suggest that what lies at the bottom of a new global circumstance of proliferating migrations and (racialized or other) ghettoizations is, precisely, the *business* of capital accumulation, whether in and through imperial enterprise or otherwise. So, if in telling this woman's story Serge is in some sense telling his own, then Rhys's gist is that Serge may be linked to the mulatto woman in the sense that fascist anti-Semitism is in one respect a horrible outgrowth of the ways in which capitalist societies organize labor, i.e., again, as more evidence of the perfidious ways and means of rationalization. Indeed, Serge, we must remember, is a Russian and not a German Jew, and the Russian persecution of Jews begins only after WWII. Presumably, then, Serge is a Russian refugee so that readers who discern the novel's treatment of persecution, refugeeism, and migration extend these formations' applicability beyond the context of fascism (even if as a Jew Serge's character also resonates within the context of the novel's treatment of European fascism). Again, Rhys is preoccupied in this novel with consolidations of dictatorial leadership and patterns of political submission across the board, and, as well, more narrowly in terms of a consolidating global market, automatization in general. Thus Sasha's sense that she is spectacle, a "sad circus-lioness," and so forth—and interludes such as the following:

He loved popular fairs, this boy—the Neuilly fair, the Montmartre fair [. . . .]

One day he said: 'I'll take you to see something rather interesting' and, wandering along the streets at the back of the Halles, we came to a café where the clients paid for the right, not to have a drink, but to sleep. They sat close-pressed against each other with their arms on the table, their heads in their arms. Every place in the room was filled; others lay along the floor. We squinted in at them through the window. 'Would you like to go in and have a look at them?' he said, as if he were at exhibition of a lot of monkeys. (40)

These laborers, as dehumanized as the Martiniquean and Europe's Jews, are automatons within Rhys's global Exhibition, "spectacles" whose "'aesthetic' power" has "increase[d] with [their] increasing awkwardness and helplessness" (Chow 106).[4]

Thus, I would argue, perhaps even more compelling than the Martiniquean interlude's treatment of the problem of fascism is the way in which Sasha's "conspicuous exhibitionism" in *Good Morning, Midnight* signifies in this regard.[5] Within the context of historical fascism and its various "disciplines," Sasha's making a spectacle of herself and weeping in public and so forth amounts to counter-fascistic discourse:

> Lavabos . . . What about that monograph on lavabos—toilets—ladies? . . .
> A London lavabo in black and white marble, fifteen women in a queue,
> each clutching her penny, not one bold spirit daring to dash out of her
> turn past the stern-faced attendant. That's what I call discipline. . . .
> [. . . .]
>   When I got upstairs the American and his friend has gone. 'It was
> something I remembered,' I told the waiter, and he looked at me blankly,
> not even bothering to laugh at me. His face was unsurprised, blank. (11)

Sasha, in the above, has just returned from a visit to the "lavabo" in a bar (in Paris), having rushed off because she once again dissolves into tears, thereby offending the "American" and the woman he is with, as well as, presumably, the waiter and any other customers who witness her lack of self-control. Yet, as this passage's play on the notion of "discipline" makes clear, the waiter's and patrons' disapproval of her emotion is more disturbing than Sasha's unfortunate display: within the context of fascisms founded on discourses and programs of self-control and standardization, a character who lacks personal discipline and tends to come apart at the seams is fighting the good fight.

However, to return to Serge and the Martiniquean, what we must conclude is that Rhys has taken the pains she has to plot their global migrations so as to put forward her map of "Empire." Indeed, as a set, all of those whom Sasha encounters in her flanerie are of mixed, uncertain, or multiple provenance. In what is most certainly a nod to Conrad,[6] even Sasha's Russians are never quite certainly Russians—and much is made of René and Sasha's ambiguous nationalities: "He says his name is Nicolas Delmar, which doesn't sound very Russian to me. Anyway [. . .]" (64); "He [Serge] turns at the door and, with the mocking expression very apparent, says something in Russian. At least, I suppose it's Russian" (98). Or, on the day Sasha first meets Delmar and his doctor friend, she has the following to relate:

> We stop under a lamp-post to guess nationalities. So they say, though I
> expect it is because they want to have a closer look at me. They tactfully
> don't guess mine. Are they Germans? No. Scandinavian, perhaps? No,
> the shorter one says they are Russian. (46)

Sasha is equally doubtful about René's nationality, equally suspicious of his
claims, even as he is presented as an ethnic/national hybrid anyway:

> 'I'll tell you one thing I don't believe. I don't believe you're a French-
> Canadian.'
> 'Then what do you think I am?'
> 'Spanish? Spanish-American?' (75)
> And, finally, there is the problem of Sasha herself:
> When I get downstairs the patron tells me that he wants to see my
> passport.
> [. . . .]
> What's wrong with the fiche? I've filled it up all right, haven't I?
> Name So-and-so, nationality So-and-so. . . . Nationality—that's what
> has puzzled him. I ought to have put nationality by marriage. (14)

Rhys's novel exhibits various travelers, refugees, and immigrants, all of vague
or mixed nationality/ethnicity. They range through the pages of a novel in
which references to spectacles and exhibitions abound, so that the Paris-city
of the novel is for all intents and purposes co-extensive with the world exhibition it is hosting. Paris is the Exhibition, Paris is the world, the world is the
Exhibition. Discrete cultural identities and their attendant localities crumble
and are dispersed under a new, dis-locating transnational culture of consumer-capitalism.

Good Morning, Midnight's tropes of spectacle and exhibitionism,
Sasha's running associations with the Russians and René, and Sasha's bi-
modal character (guide/tourist, seller/shopper, seducer/seduced) all point to
the disfigurations and determinations of consumerism and the global market
under which Rhys subsumes, to a certain extent, her exploration of fascism.
But what of Sasha's remembering? And what of the novel's last minor character—the man who has the room next to hers at her hotel?

RESUSCITATION

While all that has been written above establishes that *Good Morning, Midnight* is a highly anxious treatment of a market unchecked, the novel

remains, nonetheless, a flaneur text that counters its anxieties by conceptualizing solutions to modernity's challenges. That is, when Sasha thinks to herself in the closing pages of the novel that her Paris trip has helped her to "come alive" (182), it has done so because of her status as a flaneur whose urban pedestrianism is not only a present homelessness, but also an encounter with the "past, where [her] urban history and [her] own biography intersect" (Goebel 379). That is, while Sasha begins the novel "a bit of an automaton" (10) with her plan initially to forestall any remembering, "Not too much drinking, avoidance of certain cafés, of certain streets, of certain spots" (15), chance encounters with things once familiar spur recollection: "Thinking all this [how it is necessary to avoid certain spots], I pass the exact place for my afternoon drink. It's a café on the Avenue de l'Observatoire, which always seems to be empty. I remember it like this before" (15). And, as moments such as these multiply, Sasha gives in to a wholesale recapturing of her Parisian past ("remembering this, remembering that"), a feat which, in combination with her comradely encounters with persons similarly beset, contributes to her resuscitation over the course of her holiday: as she rebuilds a sense of self she comes to see herself as a member of a larger collective.[7]

Another emphatic indication that Sasha's holiday flanerie is coincident with her de-automatization concerns the nature of her relationship with the nameless man. This said, there is no question that, as is the case with Sasha's other encounters, the relationship's meanings are multiple, in some senses favorable and others not. For example, as Emery has effectively demonstrated, the nameless man is unambiguously associated with "patriarchal authority" and "fascistic terror." Indeed, given this fact, Rhys's decision to end the novel with Sasha embracing this figure means to Emery that she has ended her novel with a decided pessimistic flourish. For Emery, Sasha's sense of having "come alive" is delusional, her progress in the novel has been a negative one, and she ends her vacation thoroughly unaware of the extent of her complicity with and submission to all forms of conditioning and terroristic authority. Contributing to Emery's sense of the disturbing nature of the book's close is the fact that Sasha appears, throughout the novel, to find the nameless man frightening, even repellent. Yet, as I see it, there is another dimension of these characters' relation in the form of a salutary understanding. However, before addressing these various matters, an additional complicating factor must be addressed. Specifically, the nameless man is not simply another comrade or a figure of terror, he is also the novel's presiding "spirit" of the capitalist machine.

What Sasha decides on first seeing the man is that he is a "commis voyageur," i.e., a traveling salesman:

> The landing is empty and deserted. At this time of night there are no
> pails, no brooms, no piles of dirty sheets. The man next door has put his
> shoes outside—long, pointed, patent-leather shoes, very cracked. He
> does get dressed then. . . . I wonder about this man. Perhaps he is a
> commercial traveler out of a job for the moment. Yes, that's what he
> might be—a commis voyageur. Perhaps he's a traveler in dressing-
> gowns. (32)

Indeed, insofar as Sasha's embrace of the *commis* will occur over a series of
Molly Bloomian "yeses," he is a Bloom of sorts, one more canvasser of a type.
Even more pointedly, this *commis* is Kafka's traveling salesman, another Gre-
gor Samsa. This is so because Sasha tends to see him haunting the landing
dressed either in a blue dressing gown or a white one (hence her decision
about what, specifically, he might sell)—and this blue gown is adorned with
"black spots" —black spots that happen to resonate with very many black
spots of *cockroaches* in *Good Morning, Midnight:* "There are some black
specks on the wall. I stare at them, certain they are moving. Well, I ought to
be able to ignore a few bugs by this time" ; "I watch cockroaches crawling
from underneath the carpet and crawling back again" : "the wall was covered
with bugs, crawling slowly. I didn't mind the bugs much" ; "The musty
smell, the bugs, the loneliness, this room." Here the *commis'* spotted gown is
mentioned:

> The man who has the room next to me is parading about as usual in his
> white dressing-gown. Hanging around. He is like the ghost of the land-
> ing. I am always running into him.
>
>   He is as thin as a skeleton. He has a bird-like face and sunken, dark
> eyes with a peculiar expression, cringing, ingratiating, knowing. What's
> he want to look at me like that for? . . . He is always wearing a dressing-
> gown—a blue one with black spots or the famous white one. I can't
> imagine him in street clothes.
>
>   'Bonjour.'
>   'Bonjour,' I mutter. I don't like this damned man. . . . (14)

The *commis* certainly calls to mind a starving insect of sorts, as his skeletal
angularity ("thin as a skeleton") and strange shoes connote brittle exoskele-
tons: "long, pointed, patent-leather shoes, very cracked." In fact, as we see in
the novel's closing scene, Rhys even gives her ghost an insect's "flickering"
eyes. The novel's close takes place as follows: just preceding it, Sasha has

finally banished René once and for all, and he has left having not taken any of her money. She then undresses, goes to her door and opens it—so as to allow the nameless man to enter, something she knows will happen, as we learn—and returns to bed:

> I don't need to look. I know.
>   I think: 'Is it the blue dressing-gown, or the white one? That's very important. I must find that out—it's very important.'
>   I take my arm away from my eyes. It is the white dressing-gown.
>   He stands there, looking down at me. Not sure of himself, his mean eyes flickering.
>   He doesn't say anything. Thank God, he doesn't say anything. I look straight into his eyes and despise another poor devil of a human being for the last time. For the last time. . . .
>   Then I put my arms around him and pull him down on to the bed, saying: 'Yes—yes—yes. . . .' (189)

Despite the positive overtone of the novel's last yeses, many critics have nevertheless read this close as a representation of Sasha's final, total capitulation, as I have said. Yet, to the extent that such readings are based on a sense of Sasha's fear of the man before this scene, there is the additional evidence suggesting that her relation to him is more complicated than this. That is, despite her utterance that she doesn't "like" him (on their first encounter), her feelings are in fact more complicated, as we see in the first of the excerpts above: "I wonder about this man." Further, even when the *commis* is portrayed at his most repellent, his behavior is occasioned by his sense that Sasha has betrayed what is indeed an understanding between them. That is, Sasha arrives to her room one day to have the *commis* open his door for the sole purpose of calling her a *sale vache*:

> As I get up to the fourth floor landing the commis opens his door and puts his head out. 'Vache! Sale vache,' he says when he sees me. His head disappears and the door is slammed, but he goes on talking in a high, thin voice.
>   I take off my coat and hat and put away the scent and stocking I have just bought. All the time I am listening, straining my ears to hear what he is saying.
>   The voice stops. A loud knock. [. . . .]
>   I march to the door and fling it open.
>   The gigolo is outside [. . . .] (149)

Sasha, as we see in the above, is quite interested in the *commis'* anger, "straining to hear what he is saying." Then, on conversing with René, she discovers the reason for the *commis'* outburst—jealousy:

> '. . . . I waited up here [says René] for you nearly an hour this afternoon. I told your landlady I was a friend of yours from London. I spoke English to her. And she asked me if I'd like to wait in the room.'
> I suppose this explains the 'Vache! Sale vache!' (150)

In effect, Sasha has been debating over the course of her vacation whether or not to take the *commis* up on his (albeit unspoken) offer of companionship, an offer he makes patently clear fairly soon after her arrival:

> I have just finished dressing when there is a knock on the door. It's the commis, in his beautiful dressing-gown, immaculately white, with long, wide, hanging sleeves. I wonder how he got hold of it. Some woman must have given it to him. He stands there smiling his silly smile. I stare at him. He looks like a priest, the priest of some obscene, half-understood religion.
> At last I manage: Well, what is it? What do you want?'
> 'Nothing,' he says, 'nothing.'
> 'Oh, go away.'
> He doesn't answer or move. He stands in the doorway, smiling. ('Now then, you and I understand each other, don't we? Let's stop pretending.')
> I put my hand on his chest, push him backwards and bang the door. It's quite easy. It's like pushing a paper man, a ghost, something that doesn't exist.
> And there I am in this dim room with the bed for madame and the bed for monsieur and the narrow street outside (what they call an impasse), thinking of that white dressing-gown, like a priest's robes. Frightened as hell. A nightmare feeling. . . . (35)

There is but one more scene in the novel depicting the *commis,* or the Sasha and *commis* in concert, a meeting that takes place between the two soon after the one described in the excerpt immediately above. The *commis* is sulking in the aftermath of Sasha's brush off:

> The commis is on the landing. He scowls at me and at once goes into his bedroom and shuts the door. Well, that's all right, that's all right. If we both try hard to avoid each other, we ought to be able to manage it. (39)

The *commis* clearly serves multiple functions in the novel. As Emery and others assert, in his guise of "obscene" priest he is an important element of the text's treatments of authority and submission vis-à-vis Rhys's critique of masculinism and fascism. Further, as I have demonstrated, in his guise of Bloom and Samsa redux, he is also the text's presiding "spirit" of the global Exhibition, as it were. Indeed, in serving multiple duty in this way, his character underscores Rhys's linking of all of these formations. And, so, to be sure, in depicting Sasha's embrace of this "priest," the final scene of the novel underscores Sasha's status as a character at the center of a text concerned with multiple forms of submission.

However, even as the novel's conclusion emphasizes again the problems of complicity and submission, it indicates, as I have said, favorable meanings as well, serving to bring any number of textual polemics to a close, including that of Sasha's having "come alive." That is, Sasha and the man's understanding in combination with the crucial way in which their relation differs from her relations with René, Serge, and Delmar point to the relationship's functioning within the narrative thread of Sasha's revival. Specifically, while all the other men (the Russians and René) prove to be in some way predatory, in the sense that they are after Sasha's money (no matter their desperation and pangs of conscience), distinguishing Sasha's relationship with the *commis* is the way in which he is the only character in the text who asks "nothing" of Sasha: "At last I manage: Well, what is it? What do you want?' / 'Nothing,' he says, 'nothing.'" This "nothing," in the final analysis, characterizes their relation very well. He never tries to sell her anything; she does not know his name; they never have a conversation. Most ironically, therefore, at the same time this traveling salesman refers to the all-encompassing net of exchange in the novel, he is the single minor character in the text with which Sasha is expected to *exchange nothing*—indeed, in the final analysis, he is very likely not a *commis voyageur* at all.

We must, in short, parse each of Sasha's various types of responses to the *commis*. When she is as "[f]rightened as hell" in his presence she is struggling with her attachment to comfortable numbness, so that it is easiest for her decide that she is simply weathering the attentions of another seducer: "('Now then, you and I understand each other, don't we? Let's stop pretending.')." When she is consumed by a "nightmarish" feeling in the same instance she is resonating, as a character, within the context of the novel's treatment of submission and interpellation. Nonetheless, as we see, there is an additional dimension of her relation to him, one that pertains to her decision in embracing him to never "despise another poor devil of a human being again." Sasha, in effect, ends the novel eschewing a generalized loathing, a loathing whose fertile ground is a debilitating desperation and self-loathing pursuant to an oppressive sense of her own profound complicity, helplessness, and isolation.

As a close to this chapter, I hazard the following parsing of Sasha's series of three final yeses: Just like old times? Yes. Has Sasha proven herself complicitous, a character who refers to multiple forms of complicity, interpellation, and enforced submission? Yes. Has Sasha managed to recover from the ruins faith in herself and others? Yes.

Chapter Two
Voyage in the Dark: Unhomely

The trouble with the Engenglish is that their hiss hiss history happened overseas, so they dodo don't know what it means.
                                                                    —*Salman Rushdie,* The Satanic Verses

Voyage in the Dark (1934) is a Frankensteinian text—a monstrous conjoining of narrative fragments, constitutively intertextual. Its title refers to Woolf's *The Voyage Out* and Conrad's *Heart of Darkness* because the book's Anglo-Caribbean protagonist, Anna Morgan, is voyaging from the colonial periphery to the imperial center, from the West Indies to London. Anna introduces herself in the narrative present "lying on a sofa, reading *Nana,*" begins the story on the stage, moves next to prostitution, and finally completely loses control (and so Zola's *Nana* is another major intertext). The terms of Anna's decline thus pertain to her inability to navigate the pitfalls of gender and to her identity crisis—which includes the discovery of the incommensurability of different histories, histories once known and familiar and now strange since having been brought into juxtaposition: "Sometimes it is was if I were back there and as if England were a dream. At other times England was the real thing and out there was the dream, but I could never fit them together" (8).

The novel, told from Anna's point of view in the form of a montage-narrative, is equally interesting as an intertext in the way that many of its fragments are citations. These citations, interspersed with other types of fragments, make up the text's minute procedural montage: Anna recollects or recites bits of books, films, and advertisements; she intones popular, traditional and official admonitions and proscriptions; she records or recites portions of songs overheard or remembered; she recollects fragments of a Caribbean past, memories which are either summoned or else assail her (and Caribbean memory also occurs in the novel in extended sections of recall); and she jumbles together presently occurring events, passing perceptions, feelings, thoughts, observations, and so forth.[1] The novel's mass of fragments is then organized into another layer of montage, as the individual fragments are grouped around either an extended Caribbean memory sequence or else a block of events occurring in the present in London. The novel is thus a dual montage, a coalition of fragments and a blocked, overlaid, geotemporal montage (London-present/Caribbean-past).

Despite the fact that *Voyage in the Dark,* like *Wide Sargasso Sea,* is overtly colonial in content, postcolonial critics, even those who are Rhys specialists, often pass over the novel on the basis that it is solipsistic or that Rhys is insufficiently developed as colonial thinker before *Wide Sargasso Sea.*[2] Yet, there are many published readings belying these more skeptical critics' position. Veronica Marie Gregg, for instance, deftly demonstrates how the novel's collage of fragments is an engagement with the master narratives of empire (123), an assembling of "aspects of imperial politics and history" which, in conjunction with "contemporary cultural artifacts (such as popular songs, advertisements, films, and books)," "provide the framework through which the narrator's story is transmitted" (116). More specifically, Gregg proposes, the story's vigorous procedural montage conveys Anna's "loss of temporal (historical) referents" (115), so that "Anna's own utterances suggest that her function is hardly to *communicate* her story" (116; original emphasis). Instead, Gregg asserts, Anna's "story writes the differential in the power of language articulated by her and by the other voices in the text" (116).

In a related vein, Aparajita Sagar has demonstrated how "the novel gives us a subjectivity produced by the discourses of others and not itself the source of meaning" (64). Anna in Sagar's reading is Rhys's monster, a character whose story lies "bare the epistemic violence by which the colonized other is produced" (62). Sagar also takes up the question of Rhys's relation to European Modernism, reading *Voyage in the Dark* and *Wide Sargasso Sea* as evidence that Rhys's writing subverts dominant European post/modernist "epistemes" in general (3). In her reading of *Voyage in the Dark* in particular, she refers to the argument that Impressionism entails an aestheticization of the world and says that Rhys denaturalizes the technique in order to highlight both this dynamic, and, more particularly, the way in which Impressionism operates in the colonial texts of Conrad, Kipling, Orwell and Forster to "bestow a knowability on othered terrain" (66).

Like Sagar, I am interested in the novel's colonial diagnostics. However, rather than focusing on aspects of the text which point to Rhys's engagement with compensatory formations within Euro-Modernism, I address its periodizing intentions, the way in which, through proliferating textual uncannies, the London of the novel is constructed as a city gestating, beset by the first intimations of the complexities and implications of imperio-colonial history. Rhys's London is a city, in short, where an historical, geopolitical forgetting is just beginning to lift.[3] I approach the novel, therefore, as a paradigmatic "unhomely" text in Homi K. Bhabha's sense, as I argue that its uncannies pertain to "hauntings of history." Such an approach, certainly, sheds light on one of the novel's oddities, namely the motif of Anna's disconcerting looks and presence. Anna is a contagious presence vis-à-vis her London familiars in the novel, an hysteric who induces hysteria, a character not "all there" who is able to spread what she is hosting to those with whom she comes into contact. Read as a textual uncanny, Anna's ability to disconcert follows from her combination of familiarity and strangeness, on the way in which, in other words, in her capacity as a colonial, she agitates the uneasy bed of imperial repression—the "there" but "not all there" of metropolitan-colonial relations.[4] Further, Anna is not only a ghost of history in the novel, she is also haunted. She is, indeed, *the* representative metropolitan Briton and imperial subject in the novel. The London she circulates is perversely animated, her mood is morbid, and within her eerie hush she strains to hear and discern the meanings of beckoning presences and signs.

Voyage in the Dark's uncanny primarily rests on the "interstitial intimacy" existing between Anna's "psyche and the social"—on the way in which she is privy to "obscure signs of the spirit-world" and is in touch with "the sublime and the subliminal" (Bhabha 12):

> Private and public, past and present, the psyche and the social develop an interstitial intimacy [in unhomely texts]. It is an intimacy that questions binary divisions through which such spheres of social experience are often spatially opposed. These spheres of life are linked through an 'in-between' temporality that takes the measure of dwelling at home, while producing an image of the world of history. [. . . .] And the inscription of this borderline existence inhabits a stillness of time and a strangeness of framing that creates the discursive 'image' at the crossroads of history and literature, bridging the home and the world. (13)

That which previous critics have read as Anna's and by extension the text's solipsism may be recast in light of the above as an uncanny dissolution of the "binary divisions through which [. . .] spheres of social experience are often spatially opposed"—as Anna's myriad and extravagant hauntings, in short.

For example, we see that Anna consistently projects a macabre, death-like stillness around her:

> We got to Holloway and it was winter and the dark streets round the theatre made me think of murders. (18)

> It's funny how parts of London are as empty as if they were dead. (41)

> The big tree in the square opposite d'Adhémar's flat was perfectly still, and the forked twigs looked like fingers pointing. Everything was perfectly still, as if it were dead. (169)

The menace and eeriness conveyed by the statements above are in other instances more intense, as we see in these few selections (to which many more can be added):

> There was a black table with curly legs in the hall in that house, and on it a square-faced clock, stopped a five minutes past twelve, and a plant made of rubber with shiny, bright red leaves, five-pointed. I couldn't take my eyes off it. It looked proud of itself, as if it knew it was going on for ever and ever, as if it knew that it fitted in with the house and the street and the spiked iron railings outside. (34)

> A man and a girl were leaning against the railings in Brunswick square, kissing. They stood without moving in the shadow, with their mouths glued together. They were like beetles clinging to the railings. (34)

> The mantelpiece was very high and painted black. There were two huge dark-blue vases on it and a clock, stopped at ten minutes past three. (122)

> A month seemed like a week and I thought, 'It's June already.' (75)

> That's when you can hear time sliding past you, like water running. (113)

Around Anna things warp hideously (the people like "beetles" and the "high" mantelpiece and "huge" vases), or are menacing or cruel (the "railings," "spiked" iron railings, and "five-pointed" plant), and she appears to exist in a temporal vacuum or whirlwind of sorts (things are "perfectly still," seemingly "dead" or not moving, clocks are often stopped, and time whistles past her at warp speed). Anna also frequently thinks that she is being conspired against:[5]

Sometimes not being able to get over the feeling that it was a dream. The light and the sky and the shadows and the houses and the people— all part of the dream, all fitting in and all against me. (157)

We got to his house in Green Street and it was quiet and watching and not friendly to me. (35–6)

Next evening, we got back to Green Street about eleven o'clock. There was the light on over the sofa and the tray with drinks, and the rest of the house dark and quiet and not friendly to me. (49)

There was that damned bust [. . .] sneering away. (87)

There was that damned bust smiling away. (89)

However, what preys on Anna in her eerie, timeless hush and void is occasionally diffuse and benign, as in these representative instances where she appears merely to discern rushing presences in the silence, or the presence of secrets, which might yet be detected, in the quiet and dark:

I stared at myself for a long time, listening for the door to open. But I didn't hear a sound from the next room. There wasn't a sound from anywhere. When I listened I could only hear a noise like when you hold a shell up to your ear, like something rushing past you.

In this room too the lights were shaded in red; and it has secret feeling—quiet, like a place where you crouch down when you are playing hide-and-seek. (23)

But something about the darkness of the streets has a meaning. (57)

The haunted Anna, furthermore, communicates her experience through a provocative "strangeness of framing," a communicativeness that troubles common dispositions of knowledge:

The colours were different, the smells different, the feeling things gave you right down inside yourself was different. Not just the difference between heat, cold; light, darkness; purple, grey. But a difference in the way I was frightened and the way I was happy. (54)

I was always sad, with the same sort of hurt that the cold gave me in my chest. (15)

In *Jean Rhys's Historical Imagination,* Gregg explains textual peculiarities such as the statement immediately above as Anna's way of apprehending "experience through her senses, feelings, body, and memory" (116). She argues that statements such as these are an "important corollary" to the text's fragmentariness, in that these formations, together, point to how Anna "is structured ontologically as divided self, loss, absence, and silence—in the sense that she cannot 'communicate'" (116).[6] Or, as Coral Ann Howells has written in a related vein, "all that Anna learns through her immigrant experience is the full extent of her loss" (70). "Anna," she states, "[is imprisoned] by traditional codes which are emptied of meaning as they are translated from one society to another," laboring under "the condition of blankness attributed to [those who are] positioned outside the norms of an imperialist tradition and so deprived of their power to signify" (70). While there is no question that Anna's thinking through her senses and feelings contributes to our sense of her crippling identity crisis, this formation can be read also as another textual "sublime" within the context of the text's broad panoply of uncanny effects. In other words, we can conclude that beyond any question of lack, Anna's aporias are mustered by Rhys to convey a very particular notion of silence and loss. Anna's void, hush, hauntings, and that which is "not there" for her are provoking, weighty secrets and absences, absences that "arrest us with their intentionality and purpose," as Toni Morrison writes, "like neighborhoods that are defined by the population held away from them" (11). Hence, undoubtedly, the particular way in which Anna tends to remember her past in the novel:

> And then I tried to remember the road that leads to Constance Estate.
> [. . . .]
> I was nearly twelve before I rode it by myself. There were bits in the road that I was afraid of. The turning where you came very suddenly out the sun into the shadow; and the shadow was always the same shape. And the place where the woman with yaws spoke to me. I suppose she was begging but I couldn't understand because her nose and mouth were eaten away; it seemed as though she were laughing at me. I was frightened; I kept on looking backwards to see if she was following me, but when the horse came to the next ford and I saw clear water I thought I had forgotten about her. And now there she is. (150–2)

Anna in the above is not so much remembering as she is channeling a taunting ghost of history, the text thereby effecting a neat collapsing of past and present—a bringing together of London and the Caribbean—"And now there she is."

But Anna, as I have said, is a figure who is both haunted *and* haunting; she is both a ghost and ghosted. Indeed, as a "souciant" she unhomes herself much as she unhomes her friends:

> Obeah zombis souciants—lying in the dark frightened of the dark frightened of souciants that fly in through the window and suck your blood—they fan you to sleep with their wings and then they suck your blood—you know them in the day-time—they look like people but their eyes are red and staring and they're souciants at night—looking in the glass and thinking sometimes my eyes look like a souciant's eyes . . . (163)

> 'Where have you sprung from?' Laurie said. 'Come along up to my flat and have a drink. I live just round the corner in Berners Street.'
> 'No,' I said, 'I can't today, Laurie.' I didn't want to talk to anybody. I felt too much like a ghost. (114)

Thus, again, when Anna appears as the same "forgotten," grinning woman with "yaws," her facelessness and speechlessness indicate not merely marginality and an inability to communicate, but, additionally, an unhomely challenge of interpretation and translation as well:

> It was like letting go and falling back into water and seeing yourself grinning up through the water, your face like a mask, and seeing the bubbles coming up as if you were trying to speak from under the water. And how do you know what it's like to try to speak from under water when you're drowned? (98)

*****

Identification is a highly important motive in the mechanism of hysterical symptoms; by this means patients are enabled to express in their symptoms not merely their own experiences, but the experiences of quite a number of other persons; they can suffer, as it were, for a whole mass of people, and fill all the parts of a drama with their own personalities.

—*Sigmund Freud*, The Interpretation of Dreams

At the same time Anna is haunted, she functions in the novel as the embodi-
ment of colonial history coming home, as a material bearer of ambiguous
colonial traces and meanings. This is developed in the text through the motif
of her disconcerting looks and presence; through the way, in other words, we
are to understand that, as a colonial and creole, she is able to disturb the bed
of imperio-metropolitan repression. Why, after all, should Anna inspire the
irritation, misreadings and unduly violent reactions she does? What, Rhys
provokes her reader to ask, is the source of her "sublime"?

One particular scene in which Anna rather bizarrely rankles her inter-
locutor illuminates the significance of this motif very well. Anna at this point
is renting a room from a woman, Ethel, for whom she is also working as a
manicurist. Ethel suspects that Anna is responsible for a mishap that occurs
with a client, but Anna is scoffing. Ethel takes Anna to task, works herself up
to insulting Anna, and then throws a fit:

> 'And as a matter of fact you're enough to drive anybody crazy with that
> potty look of yours' [. . . .] 'The thing about you,' she said, 'is that
> you're half-potty. You're not all there, you're a half-potty bastard. You're
> not all there; that's what the matter with you. Anybody's only got to
> look at you to see that.' (145)

These words point to a rationale for Ethel's loss of control. Of note first is
that, by having Ethel accuse Anna-the-Creole of being "half-potty" and a
"bastard" and say it's written all over Anna's face, Rhys wishes us to understand that Ethel is summoning racist science. In other words, what Ethel
really is trying to say is that Anna is "potty" because she's a bastard, half-
white and half-black (even as Anna's racial provenance is left ambiguous in
the novel). Of further interest is Ethel's second way of referring to Anna's
putative madness: Anna is "not all there." This can only be a small joke on
the part of Rhys in the form of a *double entendre:* Anna is not "all there"
because she is taken with, taken by, and a signifier of, "elsewhere." Of note
last is Anna's contagiousness, the way in which she sympathetically triggers
an unhomely consciousness of not-all-thereness: "'you're enough to drive
anybody crazy with that potty look of yours.'" All told, Ethel's hysterical outburst conveys the following: Anna in relation to this minor character embodies the fact of repressed, "intimate" relations between peoples; Anna
unhomes Ethel—Ethel is beset by estranging intimations of the "colonial
repressed" which she herself cannot understand.

To the incident above we can connect the other odd, related moments
in the novel. For example, a bit earlier in the text, a different acquaintance

informs Anna that she doesn't look all there. But to this acquaintance Anna doesn't look mad so much as dreamy or far-away—"half-asleep." Further, the note of contagion is sounded once again: "you always look half-asleep"—"and people don't like that" (129). Or, a few pages after Ethel's outburst, a man visiting the salon tells Anna that her (half-asleep? souciant?) eyes look not so much far-away in a sleepy way, but far-away in a drugged way:

> When he kissed me he said, 'You don't take ether, do you?'
> 'No,' I said, 'that's a face-lotion I use. It has ether in it.'
> 'Oh, that's it,' he said. 'You know, you mustn't be mad with me, but you look a bit as if you took something. Your eyes look like it.' (153–4)

The inception of this odd, unhomely motif occurs early on in the text. Anna is first accused of being, if not looking, "potty," by a chorus girl acquaintance in a scene that takes place in Anna's boarding-house rooms, where she is being kept at this point by a London banker. Maudie, the friend, is struck by unwelcome, disturbing intimations of the "spirit world" beyond:

> [Anna] said 'I don't like London. It's an awful place; it looks horrible sometimes. I wish I'd never come over here at all.'
> 'You must be potty,' Maudie said. 'Whoever heard of anybody who didn't like London?' Her eyes looked scornful.
> 'Well, everybody doesn't,' I said. 'You listen to this thing.' I got it [a poem left by the previous boarder] and read:
> [. . . .]
> 'Hey,' Maudie said, 'that's enough of that.'
> I began to laugh. I said, 'That's the man who had these rooms before me. The landlady told me about him. She had to chuck him out because he couldn't pay his rent. I found these things in a drawer.'
> 'He must have been up the pole,' Maudie said. 'D'you know, I thought there was something about this place that gave me the pip; I'm awfully sensitive like that. Anybody funny around—I always feel it in a minute. And besides, I hate high ceilings. (46–7)

Within the context of the motif of Anna's disconcerting presence, Maudie's uncanny suggests that she is sensing more than the "aura" of the embittered, impoverished indigent who had the room before Anna. Rather, what gives her the pip is Anna and Anna's mocking laughter, the way in which Anna provokes the need to reconceive the relation between "London" and the world.

Anna, then, is both haunted and haunting, and to the extent that she is haunted, she must be grouped on one level with her metropolitan counterparts—with Maudie and Laurie and the others. In other words, Anna as a character and a psychology must be approached beyond the contexts of homelessness and imperial subjectification because she serves Rhys not only as a colonial, but also as a representative Briton in the text. In the end, it becomes clear that all of Rhys's characters in *Voyage in the Dark* are fitfully unhomed.[7]

*****

In fact it is very difficult to appreciate the full value of the various elements [of automatic writing] when confronted by them. It can even be said to be impossible to appreciate them at the first reading. These elements are outwardly <u>as strange to you who have written them as to anyone else</u>, and you are naturally distrustful of them. Poetically speaking, they are especially endowed with a very high degree of <u>immediate absurdity</u>. The peculiarity of this absurdity, on closer examination, comes from their capitulation to everything—both inadmissible and legitimate—in the world, to produce a revelation of a certain number of premises and facts generally no less objective than any others.

—*André Breton*, The First Surrealist Manifesto

Now only a few features remain, which I can assign neither to Irma nor to her friend; pale, puffy, false teeth. The false teeth led me to the governess; I now feel inclined to be satisfied with bad teeth. [. . . .] What is the meaning of the fact that I have exchanged her for her friend in the dream?

The dream, in short, is one of the detours by which repression can be evaded; it is one of the principal means employed by what is known as the indirect method of representation in the mind. The following fragment from the history of the treatment of a hysterical girl is intended to show the way in which the interpretation of dreams plays a part in the work of analysis.

—*Sigmund Freud*, Fragment of an Analysis of a Case of Hysteria (Dora)

Anna's uncannies and contagiousness tell us that her narrative and character convey not only the experience of colonial unbelonging but also that of metropolitan unhomeliness. She is not "all there" because the relation between colonial periphery and metropolitan center is as yet insufficiently conceived; her uncanny presence and haunting suggest both the persistence—and the first nascent lifting—of a repression. The text's disjunctive geotemporal montage, in relation to the text's uncannies, as I shall now argue, signals explicitly the nature and challenge of the recognition that must replace the repression, namely that "difference relates," as Fredric Jameson would say. In other words, that which does not seem to be connected (here London and the Caribbean) *must* be connected (31). For Jameson, specifically collage within Postmodernism (as opposed to within Modernism) is an aesthetics of "difference relates," a response to the fact that to "cognitively map" experience within the new globalism entails not simply historical knowledge, but also the ability to synthesize information stemming from "different time-zones or from unrelated compartments of the social and material universe" (373). This is like being able to make a connection, in Jameson's example, between "an oil spill in Alaska" and "the latest Israeli bombing or search and destroy mission in Southern Lebanon":

> What I want to argue is that the tracing of such common "origins"—henceforth evidently indispensable for what we normally think of as concrete historical understanding—is no longer exactly a temporal or a genealogical operation in the sense of older logics of historicity or causality. The "solution" to a juxtaposition—Alaska, Lebanon—that is not yet even a puzzle until it is solved—Nasser and Suez!—no longer opens up historiographic deep space or perspectival temporality of the type of a Michelet or a Spengler [. . .]. (374)

Yet, of course, collage within the work of a modernist thinking globally might also be an aesthetic of "difference relates." The text's/Anna's disruptive inter-cutting between London and the Caribbean functions in addition to representing Anna's paralyzed suspension "between two different signifying systems" (74).[8] It is disjunction deployed, additionally, to coax the reader to (re)conceive the relation between colony and London.

Rhys's reader is alerted to the problem of unrepresented geohistorical relations thanks to the Freudian apparatus accompanying the London/Caribbean fragment alternations, owing to, more specifically, the way in which Anna's utterances are presented in the text as the royal road to the imperial-metropolitan unconscious: Anna frequently says that she's living in a dream; the text's jarring conjunctions of past and present are packaged to resemble "dream-thought"; in communicating irrationally Anna speaks more truthfully than she would if she were making sense. Thus, when Anna announces at the start of the novel that her "dream" is her inability to "fit" London and the Caribbean "together," she is not simply saying that she doesn't "fit" in, is homeless. She is additionally offering us material that we must decode and decipher, recalling in her hapless stead her informing evasions and elisions. *Voyage in the Dark,* in other words, is written as a novel requiring a readerly willingness to probe contradictions, look for hidden and buried meanings, and heed the hauntings of history.

One London/Caribbean alternation that illuminates this dynamic particularly well occurs near the end of Part One of the novel, roughly halfway through. (*Voyage in the Dark* has four parts: a first longest part; two shorter, equal-in-length parts; and an ending coda. Each of the first three parts is divided into numbered sub-sections.) Anna at this point in the narrative suspects that the London banker who has been keeping her has been engineering the end of their relationship. Yet, appropriately enough, she is in denial, trying very hard to repress the truth of her situation. Her denial is finally dispelled, however, when she receives a letter from the banker Walter Jeffries's cousin, Vincent Jeffries, telling her in so many words that she won't be seeing Walter again. What happens is that Anna arrives to her pension room one day, espies the letter from Vincent on her table, but does not recognize the cousin's script: "I got upstairs. It was lying on the table, and right across the room I thought, 'Who on earth's that from?' because of the handwriting" (91). These words close the seventh sub-section of Part One, and the next, penultimate segment opens with an ellipsis that ushers in a memory of the West Indies:

8

. . . I was walking along the passage to the long upper verandah which ran the length of the house in town—there were four upstairs bedrooms two on either side of the passage—the boards were not painted and the knots in the wood were like faces—Uncle Bo was in the verandah lying on the sofa his mouth was a bit open—I thought he's asleep and I started to walk on tiptoe—the blinds were down all except one so that you could see the broad leaves of the sandbox tree—I got up to the table where the magazine was and Uncle Bo moved and sighed and long yellow tusks like fangs came out of his mouth and protruded down to his chin—you don't scream when you are frightened because you can't and you don't move either because you can't—after a long time he sighed and opened his eyes and clicked his teeth back into place and said what on earth do you want child—it was the magazine I said—he turned over and went to sleep again—I went out very softly—I had never seen false teeth before not to notice them—I shut the door and went away very softly down the passage . . .

I thought, 'But what's the matter with me? That was years and years ago, ages and ages ago. Twelve years ago or something like that. What's this letter got to with false teeth?'

I read it again:

My dear Anna,
This is a very difficult letter to write [. . .]. (91–2)

The letter is presented to the reader in full, complete with its worried post-script: "*P.S. Have you kept any of the letters Walter wrote to you? If so you ought to send them back*" (94). The text of this letter is immediately followed by Anna wondering, once again, why she has remembered what she has: "'I thought, 'What the hell's the matter with me? I must be crazy. This letter has nothing to do with false teeth'" (94). But, as she relates it, she "went on thinking about false teeth, and then about piano-keys and about that time the blind man from Martinique came to tune the piano and then he played and we listened to him sitting in the dark with the jalousies shut because it was pouring with rain and my father said, 'You are a real musician'" (94).

By the time Anna shakes herself out of her past, hours have passed: "When I looked at the clock it was a quarter-past five. I had been sitting there like that for two hours" (95). While the book presents Anna seeing the letter at the end of one section and the next section opening with a memory, a properly reconstructed series of events is that Anna sees the letter, reads it, and is only then thrown into—or assailed by—her past. She then questions the timing and aptness of the memory, re-reads the letter, and is thrown into her past once again.

Significant, first, is the manner in which the memory reads more like a dream. The placement of bedrooms and the nature of the unpainted boards are not related lovingly, or with distaste, or with nostalgia. Rather, information is conveyed in a mode of flat documentary recall characteristic of persons relating portions of dreams whose details they cannot even begin to sensibly relate to. The feeling of dream is achieved also by the memory's opening image of a walk along a "passage" in relation to another long, narrow way (the "long verandah"), as this imagery evokes a psychic space seemingly more remote than that of memory, and a process of psychic tunneling more strenuous than that required by memory's operations. Consolidating the memory's dream-like nature are the weird details of wood knots looking like faces and what appears to the young Anna to be the metamorphosis of a human being into an animal. Walks through long passages, knots of wood looking like faces, fangs, paralysis, piano keys, blind men—this imagery, so condensed, reads like one of Freud's lists of object condensations in the *Interpretation of Dreams,* or like a montage sequence from one of the period's surrealist film scripts.[9]

Also significant about this instance of montage is the way that the memory is put forward as a substitute for the letter, something whose meaning is roughly equivalent to the letter's, since it is placed in the text where the letter should be. It is thus Anna's hectic "interpretation" of her circumstances, that which occurs to her after reading it in lieu of reasoned, self-conscious reflection. Yet, this "interpretation" is thoroughly coded, its meaning, certainly, inaccessible even to her: "'What the hell's the matter with me? I must be crazy. This letter has nothing to do with false teeth.'" This London-Caribbean alternation, in sum, tells us that Anna is communicating an insight she neither quite grasps in itself nor in its implications, her jarring conjoining of false teeth and letter pointing to what Theodor Adorno ascribes in general to the dynamic of "shock and montage in surrealism": the "sensory apparatus of the individual is traumatized by the discovery that the rational is actually irrational" (440). Furthermore, since Anna herself, so ostentatiously, cannot make the necessary connections and so communicate her discovery, this task is left begging for the reader, a reader who, as Rhys undoubtedly hoped, would rise to the occasion and approach the task of deciphering as a geopolitical exercise in making "difference relate."[10] (These connections are discussed below.)

*****

A legacy is not something you can give or take by choice, and there are no certainties in the sticky business of inheritance.

—*Zadie Smith*, White Teeth

A look at one last unhomely detail will demonstrate the extent to which the trope of repression/recognition governs this novel. This detail is the character of Anna's stepmother, Hester, whose name refers to the hysteria and the disfiguring repression she is hosting.

Hester, we are informed, was married to Anna's father in England while he was on a visit there following his first wife's death. We learn that Hester detested the Caribbean and returned to England no sooner than the last shovelful of dirt was heaped onto her husband's grave. She is, as Gregg writes, a "self-appointed representative of British cultural supremacy," a woman whose speech both evokes and parodies European travel narratives' "construction of the English gentlewoman who visited or lived in the West Indies" (123–4). She is, indeed, the text's most glaring mouthpiece of imperial prejudice; she is (repressed) Imperial Britannia personified, in short.

Hester appears in the novel over the course of an extended London sequence in which Caribbean memory introjections also occur (we first meet Anna's Uncle Bo, the primary "clue" in the letter-memory cipher above, in one of these introjections). The scene takes place in a boarding house where Hester has come from the country. Her intention, although Anna doesn't know it, is to cut off entirely the already strained and infrequent relations she has with her stepdaughter. Her decision to do so follows from her receipt of a letter from Anna's Uncle Bo (or Ramsay), in which, since she suggested that Anna return to the West Indies, Ramsay writes back saying to send Anna by all means, as long as she arrives with her share of the monies Hester received from the sale of her husband's estate, Morgan's Rest:

> 'And all the thanks I get is this outrageous charge that I've cheated you and all the responsibility for the way you're going must be put on my shoulders. Because don't imagine that I don't guess how you're going on. Only some things must be ignored some things I refuse to be mixed up with I refuse to think about even. And your mother's family stand aside and do nothing. I shall write once more to your uncle and after that I shall have no further communication with your mother's family whatever. They always disliked me,' she said, 'and they didn't trouble to conceal it but this letter is the last straw.' (63–4)

In the above, Hester's defining hysterical symptom, run-on speech, is detectable precisely in the sentence that tells us she has a problem with repression: "'Only some things must be ignored some things I refuse to be mixed up with I refuse to think about even.'" These additional following passages confirm Rhys's particular treatment of Hester, as they contain the information readers require in order to understand Rhys's rationale for Hester's hysteria:

> '. . . . The way English people are cheated into buying estates that aren't worth a halfpenny is a shame. Estate! Fancy calling a place like that an estate. Only I must say that your father ought to have known better after thirty years out there and losing touch with everybody in England. Once he said to me, "No, I never want to go back. It cost me too much last time and I didn't really enjoy it. I've got nobody there who cares a damn about me. The place stinks of hypocrites if you've got a nose," he said. "I don't care if I never see it again." When he said that I knew he was failing. And such a brilliant man poor man buried alive you might say yes it was a tragedy a tragedy. But still he ought to have known better

than to have let himself be cheated in the way he was cheated first and last. Morgan's Rest! Call it Morgan's Folly I told him and you won't be far wrong. Sell it! I should think I did sell a place that lost money and always has done and always will do every penny of money that anybody is stupid enough to put into it and nothing but rocks and stones and heat and those awful doves cooing all the time. And never seeing a white face from one week's end to the other and you growing up more like a nigger every day. Enough to drive anybody mad. . . .' (62)

Bewildered by Hester's outburst, Anna thinks: "I had been expecting something so different that what she was saying didn't seem to make any sense" (62). Hester goes on:

> '[Ramsay a] gentleman! With illegitimate children wandering about all over the place called by his name—called by his name if you please. Sholto Costerus, Mildred Costerus, Dagmar. The Costeruses seem to have populated half the island in their time it's too funny. And you being told they were your cousins and giving them presents every Christmas and your father had got so slack that he said he didn't see any harm in it. He was a tragedy your father yes a tragedy and such a brilliant man poor man. But I gave Ramsay a piece of my mind one day I spoke out I said, "My idea of a gentleman an English gentleman doesn't have illegitimate children and if he does he doesn't flaunt them." "No I bet he doesn't," he said, laughing in that greasy way—exactly the laugh of a negro he had—"I should think being flaunted is the last thing that happens to the poor little devils. Not much flaunting of that sort done in England." Horrible man! How I always disliked him!. . . .'
>   'Unfortunate propensities,' she said. (64–5)

As Hester babbles on not making "any sense," Anna reports, quite appropriately, that Hester "had started talking slowly, but it now seemed as if she couldn't stop. Her face was red. 'Like a rushing river, that woman,' as Uncle Bo used to say" (64). This comment of Anna illuminates the reason why Bo/Ramsay is the crucial clue in the letter-memory interlude above: Anna identifies with her uncle and thinks of him only with fondness, despite his assumption that Black women are at his sexual disposal. Thus, her blind spot and the (geohistorical) connection the reader must make between the Jeffries/London and Ramsay/colony fragments is that the Jeffries's actions are underwritten by the same intersecting ideologies of gender, class *and* race that guarantee Walter's eventual eschewal of her, as in becoming his mistress she has become Walter's illicit, "*beastly love*" (93; original emphasis). Or, to put this another way, Rhys's "geohistorical" point is that imperialism informs metropolitan constructions of femininity, so that British middle-class womanhood becomes all the more ethereal as Blacks and under-class women are dehumanized.[11]

But, to return to the present point, the passages above confirm once again the rationale behind Rhys's continuous and unhomely play with the tropes of repression and recognition. Hester is a character whose every instinct is to repress and deny: She can barely tolerate the thought of her stepdaughter and sees her as little as possible. Her idea has been to ship Anna to the West Indies, removing her completely from sight and mind. Short of this, she will cut off relations with Anna and her West Indian connections entirely, proclaiming, in the process, that she is in no way responsible for Anna. Clearly opposing Hester, then, is Anna's father and Uncle Ramsay, both of whom refuse not to think, not to hide, or not to get "mixed up." Thus, Hester's late husband is characterized by his dislike of England and his claim that it "stinks of hypocrites," while Uncle Bo does not bother to "conceal" his dislike of Hester and "flaunts" his illegitimate mixed-race children for all to see. And so on. The substance of the Hester interlude, in short, turns on the oppositions of the hidden versus the seen, the repressed versus the recognized, the separation and hierarchy of cultures and races versus complex, complexly generative cultural and racial interrelations.

"Enough to drive anybody mad," Hester declares in her maddened, hysterical speech. This is Anna and Anna's interlocutors' same madness, hauntings and aporias pointing to the problem of metropolitan imperial denial in *Voyage in the Dark*. This third of Rhys's novels thus explores the unhomely event of colonial history coming home, of finding oneself a traveler not abroad but in one's own home. Anna therefore is not only the Creole, homeless Anna, but she is also a "Morgan," a representative scion of British, mercenary, colonial excursions abroad (her naming invokes Henry Morgan, who began a Caribbean career as a buccaneer and was subsequently employed by the British Crown first as a mercenary and then as a naval captain, and who was, finally, rewarded for his services with a tenure as Governor of Jamaica). Anna Morgan is every metropolitan Briton in *Voyage in the Dark,* as unhomed as Maudie or Laurie, and the haunted house of London through which she treads houses this whole host of haunted dreamers. They are characters all beset by disconcerting intimations of the colonial theater behind the metropolitan curtain of silence; characters all unhomed by intimations of a postcolonial beyond.

Chapter Three

Rhys/Deleuze—Rhys/Conrad: *After Leaving Mr. Mackenzie, Almayer's Folly,* and the Problem of Masochism in Rhys

He had definitely suspected her of hoarding some rather foolish letters which he had written and which she had insisted that she had torn up. One of the letters had begun, 'I would like to put my throat under your feet.' He wriggled when he thought of it. Insanity! Forget it; forget it.

—*ALMM*

The singer—a drably vague figure standing as near as he dared to the entrance to a public bar—had started The Pagan Love Song for the second time.

—*ALMM*

The well-known shrill voice startled Almayer from his dream of a splendid future into the unpleasant realities of the present hour.

—*Joseph Conrad,* Almayer's Folly

This chapter unfolds in a number of related sections. First, the body of criticism exploring the question of Rhys's protagonists' masochism is addressed to the end of complicating its terms. This has been an area of debate in the criticism because many, if not all, readers of Rhys find fault with the modernist period novels, perceiving patterns of victimization in the female protagonists' thoughts and actions above and beyond that which corresponds to the author's feminist method of depicting female gender conformity. "Passive" and "victims" are the common terms employed in the criticism, and the characters' excessive passivity is usually said to point to Rhys's complicity with that which she otherwise critiques. As for critics who launch defenses of the characters, they tend not to deny the characters' overweening victimhood.

They assert instead that the characters represent a realism of female gender subordination, no matter how obsessively or bleakly rendered. This chapter complicates the terms of this debate with a theory of masochism as yet unconsidered in the criticism, one arguing that the complex does not in fact indicate submission but rather involves a *contestation* of oppressive authority. I explore Rhys's writing in terms of this other theory of masochism, focusing particularly on Rhys's second novel, *After Leaving Mr. Mackenzie,* which I propose is the most thoroughly masochistic of her fictions. I then demonstrate that there is colonial subtext in *After Leaving Mr. Mackenzie* by illuminating the way in which it is written after (what I argue is) the equally masochistic *Almayer's Folly.* In other words, I read the masochistic valences of these two texts as oppositional formations, which in Conrad's case are mustered to particularly anti-imperial ends and in Rhys's case to these and feminist ends.

THE DEBATE

Coral Ann Howells has presented the most recent and most developed argument that Rhys's early protagonists' masochism exceeds any reasonable feminist intent, utilizing the work of Rachel Blau Du Plessis in her discussion of the problem. Howells cites Du Plessis's observation that the work of so many modernist feminist writers evinces a "movement between complicity [with] and critique [of]" traditional gender norms, proposing that Rhys's complicity is evident in the way that her women, despite their awareness "of the social structures within which they are trapped," "do not attempt to break out" of them (Howells and Du Plessis qtd 13). Instead, Howells says, "they assiduously try to stay within the condition of their entrapment, where every new instance of betrayal represents another expulsion from paradise" (13).

Howells stresses, in particular, Du Plessis's notion of "romantic thralldom" in regards to female modernist ambivalence and the characters they created. In Howells's words, romantic thralldom takes "the form of romantic fantasies of falling in love as a state of self-abandonment to male mastery" (14). This corresponds to Du Plessis's definition:

> Romantic thralldom is an all-encompassing, totally defining love between apparent unequals. The lover has the power of conferring self-worth and purpose upon the loved one. Such love is possessive, and while those enthralled feel it completes and even transforms them, dependency rules. The eroticism of romantic love, born of this unequal relationship, may depend for its satisfaction upon dominance

and submission. Thralldom insists upon the differences between the sexes or partners, encouraging a sense of mystery surrounding the motives and powers of the lover. Because it begins and ends in polarization, the sustenance of different spheres is both a cause and an effect of romantic love. Viewed from a critical, feminist perspective, the sense of completion or transformation that often accompanies such thralldom has the high price of obliteration and paralysis. This kind of love is socially learned, and it is central and recurrent in our culture. (66–7)

Du Plessis elaborates on this type of love primarily in terms of the poet H.D., whose mystical work, she believes, shows this problem of "female thralldom" occurring with "dismal frequency" (67). Howells's accurate but less elaborate definition of romantic thralldom is perhaps fitting for a treatment of Rhys, since any thralldom in Rhys's novels does not resemble the spiritual heterosexualism found in the work of H.D., D.H. Lawrence, and other modernists like them. For Howells, indeed, thralldom in Rhys is closer to a "version of female Gothic," with Rhys often presenting, she argues, "the female victim complex as a distinctive construct of the feminine, and "where Gothic fantasizing becomes itself a mechanism of defense against reality" (19–20).

For Howells, then, and critics like her, Rhys's feminist exposé of gender conformity unfortunately conveys, as well, a disturbing attachment to the status quo:

> Though her novels may be read as offering a radical critique of sexual power politics, it could equally well be argued that in her retelling of romance plots which always end in women's betrayal and failure, she speaks to women's deepest insecurities, just as her stories of women's rage at social and sexual injustice and their silence may be read as confirming women's deepest fears. (20)

On the other side of this debate are critics such as Mary Lou Emery, whose argument in defense of Rhys's feminist method stands out for its historical underpinnings. Specifically, she proposes that Rhys's focus on the ways and means of women's subjugation is best understood within the context of a contemporaneous debate about female masochism, in which Karen Horney, most notably, was arguing a theory by way of contesting the predominant Freudian view that masochism is a core component of normal femininity. For Freud, that is, a universal "female masochism" was understood to be the result of the suppression of women's natural aggressiveness, as cultural norms and biology interact so that women perceive themselves as the lesser sex and confer dominance on men. Thus, as Freud argued, whereas a little boy's fear of castration results in the setting up of a "severe super-ego," a little girl's tractability follows at best from shame and mortification, since she is and knows she is already "castrated." In developing a socially acceptable "preference for passive aims," as Freud argued, which "playing the passive part in coitus" reinforces, women manage their aggression (by directing it inwards) and perform their inferiority through masochism:

> The suppression of women's aggressiveness which is prescribed for them constitutionally and imposed on them socially favours the development of powerful masochistic impulses, which succeed, as we know, in binding erotically the destructive trends which have been diverted inwards. Thus masochism, as people say, is truly feminine. ("*Femininity*" 116)

For Freud, that is, masochism in the "*Economic Problem of Masochism*," his major paper on the subject, is actually *sadism* turned inward upon the self: "We should not be astonished to hear that under certain conditions the sadism of the destruction instinct which has been directed outwards can be introjected, turned inward again, regressing in this way to its earlier condition" (262).

While conforming to Freud's view that masochism indicates submission and/or some type of self-censure, feminists such as Karen Horney, as Emery points out, were quick to contest Freud's biological rationale for female masochism, arguing instead that social conditions entirely "generate the attributes of clinically diagnosed masochism" (116). These attributes, according to Horney, are:

> an inhibited and emotionally dependent personality; a weak and helpless self-image; the use of weakness and helplessness in struggles for power and as reasons for special consideration; and the tendency to behave submissively, to be and feel exploited, to confer responsibility on men. All of these symptoms are aspects of the masochistic tendency 'to arrange in fantasies, dreams or in the real world, situations that imply suffering; or to feel suffering in situations that would not have this concomitant for the average person.' (Emery 115–6; and Horney qtd in Emery)

Emery's point is that Rhys's women exhibit traits that correspond to *this* version of "feminine masochism." Thus, as she says, Rhys's texts very clearly explore and critique "the specific social conditions that create an insecure and dependent ego in women" (116):

I am not arguing that Rhys read Horney's papers or followed the debate I have described; I think the questions posed by the debate were available to her through the cultural climate in which she wrote, and her Caribbean background provided insight into racial and sexual power relations that opened to dialogic questioning in her writing any official conclusions about feminine masochism. (118–9)

The problem of (female) masochism in Rhys remains a sticking point in the criticism. Any given textual detail will constitute a devastating portrayal of a woman internalizing and playing out misogyny for one critic, while to the next it will be this *as well as* evidence of Rhys's disturbing commitment to traditional female submissions.

RHYS/DELEUZE

> The "demonstrative" or, more accurately, the persuasive feature (the particular way in which the masochist exhibits his suffering, embarrassment and humiliation).
>
> —Gilles Deleuze, Masochism

As the terms of the debate about Rhys suggest, critics who perceive female masochistic complicity in Rhys believe that it is intertwined with her feminist project of exposé. In other words, what they believe is that, in focusing so intensely on female submission, Rhys reveals her true colors: she derives satisfaction from depicting her women in a humiliating light, and this inspires readerly recoil and confusion.

A look at a few representative passages of submission/masochism in Rhys's early texts is in order. This one, from Rhys's third novel *Voyage in the Dark,* depicts the principal female character and narrator, Anna Morgan, kissing the hand that oppresses her. Even as the passage makes it clear that Anna is being groomed into what will be her new role of kept woman, Rhys's particular treatment of the circumstances of Anna's humiliation seems untoward and too painfully drawn out:

> He came into the room again and I watched him in the glass. My handbag was on the table. He took it up and put some money into it. Before he did it he looked towards me but he thought I couldn't see him. I got up. I meant to say, 'What are you doing?' But when I went up to him, instead of saying, 'Don't do that,' I said. [sic] 'All right, if you like—anything you like, any way you like.' And I kissed his hand.

'Don't,' he said. 'It's I who ought to kiss your hand, not you mine.'
I felt miserable suddenly and utterly lost. 'Why did I do that?' I thought.
But as soon as we were out in the street I felt happy again, and calm and
peaceful. We walked along in the fog and he was holding my hand. (38–9)

In another scene from this same novel, Anna once again appears to us, up
close and personal, exhibiting the ways and means of her debasement—even
if in a somewhat different light:

I said, 'Good night, Germaine. Good night, Vincent; thank you very
much.' What did I say that for? I thought. I'm always being stupid with
this man. I bet he'll make me feel I've said something stupid.
And sure enough he raised his eyebrow, 'Thank me very much? My
dear child, why thank me very much?' (87)

Again, as in *Good Morning, Midnight,* the reader must read through one
scene of humiliation after another. Here, for example, the principal character, Sasha Jensen, is recalling an attempt she made in the past to pick up a
man:

I start to giggle. He runs his hand up and down my arm.
I say: 'Do you know what's really the matter with me? I'm hungry.
I've had hardly anything to eat for three weeks.'
'Comment?' he says, snatching his hand away. 'What's this you're
relating?'
'C'est vrai,' I say, giggling still more loudly. 'It's quite true. I've had
nothing to eat for three weeks.' (Exaggerating, as usual.)
At this moment a taxi draws up. Without a word he gets into it, bangs
the door and drives off, leaving me standing there on the pavement. (90)

From the same novel:

Last night for instance. Last night was a catastrophe.
[. . . .]
. . . The woman at the next table started talking to me -
[. . . .]
She was waiting for a friend, she told me.
The friend arrived—an American. He stood me another brandy-
and-soda and while I was drinking it I started to cry.
I said: 'It was something I remembered.'

> The dark woman sat up very straight and threw her chest out.
> 'I understand,' she said, 'I understand. All the same. . . . Sometimes I'm just as unhappy as you are. But that's not to say that I let everybody see it.' (9–10)

This particular set of passages from Rhys's novels highlights an additional way in which we might approach masochistic scenes in Rhys, seeing her as a writer highly interested in *letting "everybody see it"*—that is, as a writer interested in *representing humiliation per se*—as opposed to, more narrowly, a writer interested in depicting females being submissive.[1] In other words, I am asserting that Rhys's particular feminist focus on female masochism/gender conformity is partially underwritten by a commitment to the writing of humiliating display. This suggestion follows from a review of the literature on masochism in which we find, again and again, theorists' point that a core component of the masochistic enterprise, literary or otherwise, is *exhibiting* suffering and embarrassment, that which since Theodor Reik's work on masochism has been called its "demonstrative" feature. This is a significant point in terms of Rhys because, yet more pertinently, a related and common point in the literature, if not precisely a consensual one, is that submissive display is a significant component of masochism's core feint, namely that, as sociologist Lynn Chancer has put it, the masochist's "secret" is "strength and independence [. . .] hidden behind a front of apparent and extreme dependency" (59).

In Gilles Deleuze's major work on masochism in particular, *Coldness and Cruelty*, I find a most useful treatment of the formation in terms of Rhys. It is most useful first because he argues in straightforward terms (which I present below) this view that masochism does not indicate submission; rather he argues this "other" view of masochism I am interested in exploring in terms of Rhys here. (This does not mean, however, that I am arguing against Howells or Emery above; rather, as I have said, I am complicating the terms of the debate by concluding that at least some of what looks like complicity in Rhys is undoubtedly the overflow of this "other" masochism.) Equally compelling about *Coldness and Cruelty* is that Deleuze is not at pains to establish any etiology of masochism in terms of any real individuals' masochistic performances. Rather, Deleuze's psychoanalytics are employed to the end of exploring the varying socio-political motivations and imaginaries of the Marquis de Sade and Leopold von Sacher Masoch as these manifested in literary exercises of treatments of power—competing visions of law and order, as it were—within an historical context. Further, Deleuze discusses at length those motifs in Masoch's novels functioning as central components of the texts' masochistic investments, motifs which, as we shall see, occur prominently in Rhys's novels as well. Certainly, particularly in the excerpts from *Good Morning, Midnight* above, we can detect very easily the Deleuzian masochistic rationale.

Briefly for the moment, for Deleuze, only sadistic scenarios with their orchestrating torturers entail an inflation of the "paternal" function or of the law/superego: the goal of the sadistic torturer is to find an unwilling victim and to cause suffering and secure submission. Masochistic theaters, on the contrary, are orchestrated by the victim and pertain to a *deflation* of the punitive powers of the law: the goal is to find and groom a torturer whose punishments are denied as pain and experienced as pleasure instead. Thus the masochist in Deleuze is an oppositional figure and a fantasist—an ironist and humorist of sorts whose desperation resolves as an outwitting and disavowal of the law by, again, experiencing repression/punishment as pleasure. And, indeed, as we see above, Sasha's hyperbolic narration makes light of her suffering while ridiculing those who witness and/or contribute to it. The disconcerted man and woman are objects of fun, quite ridiculous: "'Comment?' he says, snatching his hand away. 'What's this you're relating?'"; "The dark woman sat up very straight and threw her chest out." Sasha, in fact, laughs at even herself: "Exaggerating as usual"; "catastrophe." What we see in the scenes of humiliation in *Good Morning, Midnight,* in effect, is the way in which masochistic energies are deployed in order to deny suffering and resuscitate s/he who or that which (ego) suffers. Sasha (victim/ego) and the disapproving man and woman (extensions of the law/superego) are all, ultimately, worth a "giggle" or two.

What the rest of this chapter sets out to establish, then, is that Rhys is a writer in what might best be called the Masochian tradition. To this end, I explore how masochistic formations and motifs consistently congeal, dissolve and mutate into something other in Rhys's writing, intersecting with and inflecting the novels' feminist and other investments. Thus, besides exploring masochistic valences in Rhys's writing that in no way correspond to what so far has been scrutinized as evidence of Rhys's (or her characters') masochism, this chapter will illuminate how depictions of female gender conformity in Rhys's novels meld with instances of masochistic demonstrativeness, so that, as I have said, some if not all of what feels like complicity in the novels is undoubtedly the overflow of this "other" masochism, indicating not complicity at all but rather its obverse. I accomplish this by first fleshing out in greater detail Deleuze's discussions of masochism and Masoch. Then, after applying these insights to Rhys's writing in general and to a reading of *After Leaving Mr. Mackenzie* in particular, I demonstrate in the last half of this chapter that, given the particular way in which *After Leaving Mr. Mackenzie* is written after the equally masochistic *Almayer's Folly,* there is no question that the masochistic energies in at least this of Rhys's novels are a deflation of and critical response to imperial oppressions—thus oppression generally— and not strictly gender oppression.

III

Deleuze begins *Coldness and Cruelty* by contesting the common view of the complementarity of sadism and masochism—by insisting there can be no "entity" termed "sadomasochism" (13).[2] The fundamental difference between the two regimes is indicated in his view by the fact that, no matter that the "one enjoys inflicting pain while the other enjoys suffering pain seems to be such striking proof of their complementarity," in fact, as he puts it, "the genuine sadist could never tolerate a masochistic victim"—the victim must be unwilling—and the genuine "masochist [could never] tolerate a truly sadistic torturer" (40–1).

Again, at the center of Deleuze's study are the texts of von Sacher Masoch, most particularly the various types of women found in the novels to the end of fixing the precise nature of Masoch's ideal dominatrix figure. I briefly review portions of his discussion of these women for two reasons. First, in order to demonstrate that—as in Rhys—even in Masoch a seamless masochistic order flits in and out of focus, here waxing, there waning or threatening to do so. Second, because Deleuze's description of the female "masochistic ideal" informs my analysis of recurring female character types in Rhys.

Deleuze, then, discovers three types of women in Masoch, "the hetaeric," "the masochistic ideal" and "the sadistic." He proposes that their inspiration lies in the writings of one of Masoch's contemporaries, Bachofen (52):

> Bachofen distinguished three eras in the evolution of humanity. The first is the hetaeric or Aphroditic era, born in the lustful chaos of primeval swamps: women's relations with man were many and fickle, the feminine principle was dominant and the father was "Nobody" (this phase, typified by the ruling courtesans of Asia, has survived in such institutions as temple prostitution). The second, or Demetrian era, dawned among the Amazons and established a strict gynocratic and agricultural order; the swamps were drained; the father or husband now acquired a certain status but he still remained under the domination of the woman. Finally, the patriarchal or Apollonian system established itself, matriarchy surviving in degenerate Amazonian or even Dionysian

forms. Masoch's three feminine types can easily be recognized in these three stages, the first and third eras being the limits in between which the second oscillates in its precarious splendor and perfection. (52–3)

The "masochistic ideal" and the social order to which the ideal refers thus corresponds to Bachofen's middle, gynocratic era, and Masoch's triumvirate of female types according to Deleuze represents a range of femininity in which the appearance of either the hetaeric or the sadistic woman signals the dissolution of the ideal.

Masoch elaborates on each of Masoch's female types, his glosses on the sadistic woman and the masochistic ideal being pertinent here. The sadistic woman is briefly described. She "enjoys hurting and torturing others, but it is significant that her actions are prompted by a man or otherwise performed in concert with a man, whose victim she is always liable to become" (48). Thus Wanda, of Masoch's *Venus in Furs,* who begins the book identified with the hetaeric, passes through the ideal masochistic stage and ends up sadistic when the masochistic world that the principal character Severin has taken such great pains to create, crumbles and dissolves (48–9).

As for the masochistic ideal, Deleuze pins down this "fantastic charac-ter" or "this fantasy" "by piecing together the various descriptions" of her found in Masoch's novels:

In a "*conte rose,*" *The Aesthetics of Ugliness,* he describes the mother of the family: "an imposing woman, with an air of severity, pronounced features and cold eyes, who nevertheless cherishes her little brood." Martshca is described as being "like an Indian woman or a Tartar from the Mongolian desert"; she has "the tender heart of a dove together with the cruel instincts of the feline race." Lola likes to torture animals and dreams of witnessing or even taking part in executions, but "in spite of her peculiar tastes, the girl was neither brutal nor eccentric; on the contrary, she was reasonable and kind and showed all the tenderness and delicacy of a sentimental nature." In *The Mother of God,* Madonna is gentle and gay, and yet she is stern, cold and a master torturer: "Her lovely face flushed with anger, but her large blue eyes shone with a gentle light." [. . . .] In *Moonlight* we finally come upon the secret of Nature: Nature herself is cold, maternal and severe. The trinity of the masochistic dream is summed up in the words: cold—mater-nal—severe, icy—sentimental—cruel. (50–51)

Masoch's female dominatrix/male victim scenario corresponds to Bachofen's gynocratic order, Deleuze argues, because it represents the triumph of a good "mother" in a "contractual partnership with the ego" against an "institutional superego" (130). Masoch's masochistic "formula" is thus the "humiliated father" (60), in which "the mother is identified with the law" and "the father expelled from the symbolic order" (68). This formula, as we shall see, is roughly shared by Rhys and Conrad, as the masochistic oppositionality of these writers also most often takes the form of a gendered social in which the mother/a female is substituted for the father/a male as the authority figure. Thus, again, most significant here is Deleuze's departure from Freud, and Krafft-Ebing before him (who coined the term), as masochism in his schema is not a form of sadism directed inwards upon the self and so does indicate, like sadism, the superego ascendant: "We must wonder all the more why so many psychoanalysts insist on discovering a disguised father-image in the masochistic ideal, and on detecting the person of the father behind the woman torturer" (55). To the contrary, as he puts, what is being "beaten" in masochism is the image and likeness of the father/superego:

> The masochistic ego is only apparently crushed by the superego. What insolence and humor, what irrepressible defiance and ultimate triumph lie hidden behind an ego that claims to be so weak. [. . . .] If the masochistic is lacking anything, it would be a superego and not an ego at all. [. . . .] One could say almost the opposite of the sadist: he has a powerful and overwhelming superego and nothing else. (124)

In organizing a situation in which pleasure is experienced after enduring pain, in sum, the masochist outwits, through disavowal, the law's punitive, repressive, and/or oppressive powers. Further, where masochism "is a demonstration of the law's absurdity" (88), sadism, according to Deleuze, is a story that tells how the ego,

> in an entirely different context and in a different struggle, is beaten and expelled; how the unrestrained superego assumes an exclusive role, modeled on an inflated conception of the father's role—the mother and the ego becoming its choice victims. (131)

Sade's heroines are sadistic, then, because of their "sodomitic union with the father in a fundamental alliance against the mother. Sadism is in every sense an active negation of the mother and an exaltation of the father who is beyond all laws" (60).

Also central to this argument is Deleuze's distinction between the procedures of the two regimes, a point I draw on below. Whereas sadism is "institutional," masochism is "contractual"; whereas the sadist is an "instructor," the masochist is an "educator" (19):

> [In the work of Masoch we] are no longer in the presence of a torturer seizing upon a victim and enjoying her all the more because she is unconsenting and unpersuaded. We are dealing instead with a victim in search of a torturer and who needs to educate, persuade and conclude an alliance with the torturer in order to realize the strangest of schemes. This is why advertisements are part of the language of masochism while they have no place in pure sadism, and why the masochist draws up a contract while the sadist abominates and destroys them. The sadist is in need of institutions, the masochist of contractual relations. (20)

Thus, contractual interludes are frequent in the novels of Masoch, as well as other elements, many of which, as readers familiar with Rhys's oeuvre will readily recognize, are typical of her writing as well. Since I refer to some of these motifs in my exploration of *After Leaving Mr. Mackenzie,* a summation of them is in order.[3] Masoch employs representations of a femininity of stillness or artifice, arrested movement in general, mirrors, and waiting. For example, a work of art will be a source of inspiration for the masochistic victim because s/he will see the masochistic ideal in the work, or because "the plastic arts" are rendered as that which "confer an eternal character on their subject" in their suspension of "gestures and attitudes" (Deleuze 69–70). Thus Masoch's "novels . . . display the most intense preoccupation with arrested movement; his scenes are frozen, as though photographed, stereotyped or painted" (70). Scenes in Masoch also tend to "duplicate themselves in mirrors" (70), and a "mystical play of flesh, fur and mirror" predominates (69). The masochist, further and finally, is morose, a dreamer and a fantasist. The moroseness, says Deleuze, "should be related to the experience of waiting and delay" (71), and the propensity to live in dreams follows from the fact that the masochist does not favorably transmute or negotiate an intolerable "reality," but rather rejects reality in favor of an idealized fantasy of the real: "Disavowal, suspense, waiting, fetishism and fantasy together make up the special constellation of masochism" (72).

Deleuze's historical contextualizing of von Sacher Masoch and de Sade accords with his treatment of the differing significance of the two orders. The monstrous, purely institutional conception of order conveyed by Sade's literary fantasies, says Deleuze, gestures "toward a 'republicanism' of which the French [were] not yet capable": "It is as though Sade were holding up a perverse mirror in which the whole course of nature and history were reflected, from the beginning of time to the Revolution of 1789" (37). Thus, whereas Sade's paternal erotics convey an ideal institutionalism in which the need for any and all laws has withered away, the later Masoch's literary erotics, in contrast, convey a type of perverse, late "Romanticism." Masoch, that is, as Deleuze writes, identified with minority groups who were resisting vast state corporatizations. Born in 1835, in Lemberg, Galicia, Masoch was of "Slav, Spanish, and Bohemian descent" (9). His

> ancestors held official positions in the Austro-Hungarian Empire. His father was Chief of Police of Lemberg, and as a child he witnessed prison scenes and riots which were to have a profound effect on him. His work is deeply influenced by the problem of nationalities, minority groups and revolutionary movements in the Empire, hence his Galician, Jewish, Hungarian, Prussian tales, etc. He often describes the organization of agricultural communes and the struggles of the peasants against the Austrian administration and especially against the landowners. He became involved in the Panslavic movement [. . .]. (9)

Masoch's micro-nationalist sympathies inspire his fantastical "terrible Tsarina" head-of-state, a benign despot who presides over a legal machine whose workings are designed to protect the interests of minority constituencies:

> Masoch holds a perverse mirror to all nature and all mankind, from the origins of history to the 1848 revolutions of the Austrian Empire—"The history of cruelty in love." [. . . .] Masoch liked to imagine that the Slavs were in need of a beautiful female despot, a terrible Tsarina, to ensure the triumph of the revolution of 1848 and to strengthen the Panslavic movement. "A further effort, Slavs, if you would become Republicans." (38)

In Deleuze, Masoch is an anti-imperial minoritarian whose fantastical maternal despotism smacks of retrogressive, conservative nostalgia; but, pertinently, unlike Sade's theater of law and order, Masoch's is oppositionally conceived of with respect to, if not the status quo, then inexorably concatenating historico-political forces nonetheless. Thus, the machinations of order and socialization in masochism are not that which remain to be perfected, rather that which must always be contained.

Before turning to *After Leaving Mr. Mackenzie,* this idea that Rhys is a writer in the Masochian tradition can be preliminarily substantiated by touching on a detail from *Good Morning, Midnight* and by returning briefly to the one of the excerpts (above) from *Voyage in the Dark*. In the following scene from *Good Morning, Midnight,* we see Sasha, the exhibitionist, in the guise of a masochistic dreamer *par excellent,* a fantasist whose love of art follows from its apparent ability to confer an "eternal character" on its subject. Sasha is visiting an artist's studio and will buy an artwork:

> When he [the artist's friend] has finished pictures are propped up on the floor round three sides of the room.
> 'Now you can see them,' he says.
> 'Yes, now I can see them.'
> I am surrounded by the pictures. It is astonishing how vivid they are in this dim light. . . . Now the room expands and the iron band round my heart loosens. The miracle has happened. I am happy.
> Looking at the pictures, I go off into a vague dream. Perhaps one day I'll live again round the corner in a room as empty as this. Nothing in it but a bed and a looking-glass. Getting the stove lit at about two in the afternoon—the cold and the stove fighting each other. Lying near the stove in complete peace, having some bread with pâté spread on it, and then having a drink and lying all the afternoon in that empty room—nothing in it but the bed, the stove and the looking-glass and outside Paris. And the dreams that you have, alone in an empty room, waiting for the door that will open, the thing that is bound to happen. (99–100; author ellipsis)

Surrounded completely by canvasses, or having had her surroundings miraculously transmuted into art in this way, Sasha is transported into a blissful fantasy. What she fantasizes about is another timeless world, a room-world wholly detached from the hustle without, wherein decoration is limited to a sole, reduplicating mirror, and excitement takes the sole form of waiting and suspense. And to this scene we can connect Anna of *Voyage in the Dark,* in the aftermath of her humiliating kiss of her oppressor's hand:

> 'All right, if you like—anything you like, any way you like.' And I kissed his hand.
> 'Don't,' he said. 'It's I who ought to kiss your hand, not you mine.'
> I felt miserable suddenly and utterly lost. 'Why did I do that?' I thought.
> But as soon as we were out in the street I felt happy again, and calm and peaceful. We walked along in the fog and he was holding my hand.

What is so odd about this scene—what cannot be explained with recourse to notions of female/feminine masochism but can be with recourse to Deleuze—is the way that Anna ends the scene in a dreamy, comfortable "fog," feeling, most oddly, "calm and peaceful." Indeed, related to these scenes more broadly in terms of Rhys's (early) writing (especially) is the dreaminess and moroseness of her protagonists—and the consequent heavy mood of the novels—not to mention, further, Howells's sense that Rhys's women engage in "Gothic fantasizing [so that it] becomes itself a mechanism of defense against reality." In sum, in revisiting scenes of abject display in Rhys's earlier writing, and, as well, pertinently, looking beyond such displays, what we find are motifs—and character types, moods and interrelations—which suggest Rhys's decided interest in an oppositional masochism.

AFTER LEAVING MR. MACKENZIE

> [Julia] thought: 'Of all the idiotic things I ever did, the most idiotic was sell-ing my fur coat.' She began bitterly to remember the coat she had once pos-sessed. The sort that last for ever, astrakhan, with a huge skunk collar. She sold it at the time of her duel with Maître Legros.
>
> —ALMM

> 'Well, anyway, that's a wonderful coat you have.' She felt my coat. Her little hands, with short, thick fingers, felt it; and he . . . 'Now perhaps you won't shiver so much,' he said.
>
> —VD

> The last performance of What's-her-name And Her Boys or It Was All Due To An Old Fur Coat.
>
> —GMM

At the same time that the exploration of *After Leaving Mr. Mackenzie* that now follows will demonstrate Rhys's commitment to the masochistic fantasy, it does so primarily by focusing on a limited number of the typically masochistic formations of the text. That is, while I have proposed that major indications of Rhys's attachment to the fantasy are the heavy mood of the early novels and protagonists; her particular treatment of art works in her writing, as well as her penchant for mirror imagery;[4] evidence of an interest in "contractual" relations; and, last, recurring character types which evoke, however mutably, masochistic victims and ideals (mutably because female characters waver in and out of focus as "Deleuzian" victims or ideals, or, for instance, as *female* masochists—the former two depending on how they are positioned in relation to the law in any given scene)—I touch most thoroughly in this section on contractual matters and the way in which the novel's disposition of characters is generally typical of the major character players in Rhys's intersecting feminist and masochistic theaters: her protagonist tends to appear either as a female masochist or else as a (Deleuzian) masochistic victim or ideal; the novel's male characters tend to be either villains (masculinism ascendant) or victims (the Law being beaten); the maternal figure in the text is both maternal *and* severe, evoking the masochistic ideal and functioning as an alter-ego of the female protagonist.[5] Also noteworthy is the way in which *After Leaving Mr. Mackenzie*'s masochism stands out somewhat in comparison to that of the other novels. It does so for two reasons. First, because its masochism is very obvious—indeed central to the text—in contrast to the more diffuse ways in which masochistic energies tincture the other novels, and, second, because Rhys's engagement with the fantasy in *After Leaving Mr. Mackenzie* appears to take the curious form of a *lament,* by which I mean that the fantasy is evoked as that which has always-already dissolved.

A masochistic attachment to contractual relations figures prominently in Rhys's early novels in the form of the semi-legalistic connections often in force between the women and their lovers (or former lovers), as well as in the stories' flow of *pneumatiques* and letters, many of which set up assignations and so forth. In regards to this latter element, surely more so than any other modernist writer and in a strangely anachronistic way, Rhys takes pleasure in presenting, in full, the text of the many notes and letters that pass amongst her characters. Although this is true of each of the first three novels, it is especially true of the second and third. These paper trails mark and trace the networks and nature of character relations in the novels, so that these relations and connections seem thereby to be codified. More to the point, Part I of *After Leaving Mr. Mackenzie* is in this respect exemplary, as it is an extended development of the dissolution of what has been for some time a protracted and problematic "contractual" relation.

After Leaving Mr. Mackenzie opens in Paris with the expatriate Julia Martin ensconced in a hotel, where she moved six months previously following her and the eponymous Mackenzie's parting of ways. The novel's action begins with a second break from Mackenzie, as Julia has been receiving since their parting a weekly stipend, through his lawyer, and, on the day the novel opens, she receives a note telling her that its enclosed check is her last. *After Leaving Mr. Mackenzie*'s lawyer is named nothing other than "Maître Legros," and Rhys gives us a look at one of Julia's typical weekly communications:

Madame,

Enclosed please find our cheque for three hundred francs (fcs. 300), receipt of which kindly acknowledge and oblige

> Yours faithfully,
> Henri Legros,
> per N.E. (13)

However, the real action of the narrative begins when Julia receives the missive from Legros that reads as follows:

Madame,

Enclosed please find our cheque for one thousand five hundred francs (fcs. 1,500). Our client has instructed us to make this final payment and to inform you that, from this date, the weekly allowance will be discontinued.

Kindly acknowledge receipt and oblige

> Yours faithfully,
> Henri Legros (18)

This final rupture spurs Julia to action. First, she thinks of writing to Mackenzie (and the text of her aborted letter is presented in the text). But, finally, she decides that the best course of action is to confront Mackenzie face to face, which she does that night in a restaurant to which follows him.

This scene is interesting because Julia does not, as might be expected, argue for more money or berate Mackenzie for having thrown her over in the first place. What she does, instead, is object to the way in which the weekly checks were arranged, or, as I see it, complain about the nature of her and Mackenzie's "contract." In between the particularity of Julia's complaint to Mackenzie and a scene that precedes Julia's objection in the text, masochism, contractual relations, a degraded masochism, and a degraded contractuality are all conveyed. Or, to put this another way, a masochistic regime and theater are evoked, which is quite typical of Rhys, but in *After Leaving Mr. Mackenzie* this is achieved in the curious form of a lament for that which might have been:

> At the mention of Maître Legros Mr. Mackenzie pricked up his ears, for he had only received three very businesslike communications from that gentleman, and he was rather curious to know how French lawyers manage these affairs.

> She said that Maître Legros had bullied her about letters that she had
> destroyed and possible unpleasantness that she never intended to make.
> [. . . .]
> She said that the lawyer had told his clerk to lock the door and send
> for an *agent.*
> He wondered whether to believe this, for he had a vague idea that
> locking doors is one of the things that is not legal.
> She said that he had threatened to have her deported, and had talked
> a great deal about the *police des moeurs.* (31)

Julia's final comment about the unfairness of the business is: "'Why did you
pay a lawyer to bully me?'" (32).

There is no question that Julia's hurt and resentment within the context of the legalistic contours of this interlude convey the idea of institutionalized sex-gender oppressions. There is also no question that Julia has
been degraded by these payments and so has succumbed to patterns of
"feminine masochism." At the same time, nonetheless, the epistolary and
legalistic nature of these two characters' connection is resonant of
masochistic contractuality, and it is, as I have said, explicitly connected in
the text to an erotic, masochistic scenario: as he sits in the restaurant with
no idea that Julia will shortly be appearing before him, Mackenzie thinks
of Julia as follows:

> He had definitely suspected her of hoarding some rather foolish letters
> which he had written and which she had insisted that she had torn up.
> One of the letters had begun, 'I would like to put my throat under your
> feet.' He wriggled when he thought of it. Insanity! Forget it; forget it.
>
> Caution was native to him—and that same afternoon he had placed
> the whole affair in the capable hands of Maître Legros—and he had not
> seen Julia since. (28)

Thus, as I say, this interlude's evocation of masochism (Mackenzie pin-
ioned), contractual relations (Legros's services), a degraded masochism (the
dissolution of the affair), and a degraded contractuality (Legros's bullying).

This episode, indeed the entire Part I, resonates still further in this
regard. Equally notable, for example, are the unusual power dynamics
between Julia and Mackenzie, and the nature and circumstances of a third
character Horsfield's relation to Julia as well as the restaurant scene he wit-
nesses between them. All told, this theater of Julia, Mackenzie and Horsfield
plays out as a strained masochistic tableau, with Julia attempting to assert (an

apocryphal) power over Mackenzie, with Mackenzie wavering in between his identification with Legros and his identification as a victim of Julia, and with Horsfield figuring as a potential-but-never-to-be son-substitute for Mackenzie. I quote, necessarily, at length:

> She walked in—pale as a ghost. She went straight up to Mr Mackenzie's table, and sat down opposite to him. He opened his mouth to speak, but no words came. So he shut it again. He was thinking, 'O God, oh Lord, she's come here to make a scene. . . . Oh God, oh Lord, she's come here to make a scene.'
>
> He looked to the right and the left of him with a helpless expression. He felt a sensation of great relief when he saw that Monsieur Albert [the owner of the restaurant] was standing near his table and looking at him with significance.
>
> [. . . .]
>
> Mr Mackenzie's face instinctively assumed a haughty expression, as if to say 'What the devil do you mean?' He raised his eyebrows a little, just to put the fellow in his place.
>
> Monsieur Albert moved away. When he had gone little distance, he turned. This time Mr Mackenzie tried to telegraph back, 'Not yet anyhow. But stand by.'
>
> Then he looked at Julia for the first time. She said, 'Well, you didn't expect to see me here, did you?'
>
> [. . . .]
>
> There was a second place laid on the table. She took up the carafe of wine and poured out a glass. Mr Mackenzie watched her with a sardonic expression. He wondered why the first sight of her had frightened him so much. He was now sure that she could not make much of a scene. He knew her; the effort of walking into the restaurant and seating herself at his table would have left her in a state of collapse.
>
> [. . . .]
>
> She asked, 'How's your pal, Maître Legros?'
>
> 'Very well indeed, I think,' he said stiffly.
>
> She began to talk volubly, in a low, rather monotonous voice. It was like a flood which has been long dammed up suddenly pouring forth.
>
> He listened, half-smiling. Surely even she must see that she was trying to make a tragedy out of a situation that was fundamentally comical. The discarded mistress—the faithful lawyer defending the honour of the client. . . . A situation consecrated as comical by ten thousand farces and a thousand comedies.

As far as he could make out she had a fixed idea that her affair with him and her encounter with Maître Legros had been the turning-point in her life. They had destroyed some necessary illusions about herself which had enabled her to live her curious existence with a certain amount of courage and audacity.

[. . . .]

She raised her voice. 'Why did you pay a lawyer to bully me?' she said.

Mr Mackenzie pushed away his plate. This was intolerable. He could not go on pretending to eat—not if she were going to say that sort of thing at the top of her voice.

Besides, while she was talking, a chap whom he knew, a journalist called Moon, had come with a friend, and was sitting two or three tables away. Moon was a gossip. He was talking volubly, and the friend, a thin, dark, youngish man [Horsfield], was glancing round the restaurant with a rather bored expression. At any moment the attention of these two might be attracted. Who knew to what wild lengths Julia would go?

Mr Mackenzie thought, 'Never again—never, never again—will I get mixed up with this sort of woman.'

His collar felt too tight for him. He thrust his chin out in an instinctive effort to relieve the constriction. The movement was exactly like that of a horse shying.

He looked at Julia and a helpless, imploring expression came into his eyes. His hand was lying on the table. She put her hand on his, and said, in a very low voice, 'You know, I've been pretty unhappy.'

At this change of attitude, Mr Mackenzie felt both relieved and annoyed. 'She's trying to get hold of me again,' he thought. 'But what a way to do it! My God, what a way to do it!'

He drew his hand away slowly, ostentatiously. Keeping his eyes fixed on hers, he deliberately assumed an expression of disgust. Then he cleared his throat and asked, 'Well, what exactly did you want when came in here?'

[. . . .]

A cunning expression came into Julia's face. She picked up her glove and hit his cheek with it, but so lightly that he did not even blink.

'I despise you,' she said.

'Quite,' said Mr Mackenzie. He sat very straight, staring at her.

Her eyes did not drop, but a mournful and beaten expression came into them.

'Oh, well,' she said, 'all right. Have it your own way.'

Then, to Mr Mackenzie's unutterable relief, she gathered up her
gloves and walked out of the restaurant. (28–34)

When Mackenzie nervously scans the room after Julia leaves to see if anyone
has witnessed the scene, he realizes that Horsfield has done so from the latter's quickly dropped eyes and too-studied blankness of expression: "'Hell!'
thought Mr Mackenzie, 'that chap saw'" (35). Horsfield has seen it all,
thanks to the restaurant's reduplicating mirror:

> There had been something fantastic, almost dream-like, about seeing
> a thing like that reflected in a looking-glass. A bad looking-glass, too.
> So that the actors had been slightly distorted, as in an unstill pool of
> water.
>
> He had been sitting in such a way that, every time he looked up, he
> was bound to see the reflection of the back of Mr Mackenzie's head,
> round and pugnacious—somehow in decided contrast with his deliber-
> ately picturesque appearance from the front—and the face of the young
> woman, who looked rather under the weather. He had not stared at
> them, but he had seen the young woman slapping the man's face. He
> had gathered from her expression that it was not a caress, or a joke, or
> anything of that sort.
> [. . . .]
> As she walked out of the restaurant he had turned to look after her,
> and asked, 'Do you know that woman?'
> [. . . .]
> However, Moon had been decidedly sniffy about the young woman.
> When he said, 'Oh, yes. I think I've seen her about at one time and
> another,' his tone put the strange creature so much in her place that Mr
> Horsfield felt rather ashamed of having expressed any kind of interest in
> her.
> 'A stolid sort of chap, Moon,' he thought, as he walked back down
> the boulevard, 'though jumpy on the surface. A bit of a bore, too.'
> (37–8)

Despite Horsfield's piqued interest and pretensions to reckless non-conform-
ity, he is disappointed when he finally comes face to face with Julia in the bar
in which they have both ended up:

> 'D'you mind if I sit here?' Mr Horsfield asked.
> 'Of course, why not?' she said in an indifferent voice.

> Mr Horsfield looked sideways at her. She was not so young as he had thought. (40)
>
> [. . . .]
>
> She powdered her face. He thought that, for a moment, a furtive and calculating expression came into it.
>
> [. . . .]
>
> She talked about a night-club in London which he knew had been going strong just before the war broke out. Mr Horsfield thought, 'She must be thirty-four or thirty-five if she's a day—probably older.' Of course, that explained a lot of things. (41)

On their way elsewhere, outside the bar,

> She pulled her arm away without answering. A young man passing by looked curiously at them and it flashed into Mr Horsfield's mind that they must seem like a sordidly disputing couple. If all this had happened in the daylight he would have been shamefaced and would have left her as soon as he decently could. (43)

Horsfield does not, however, quit Julia's company quite yet; instead, he suggests that they duck into a cinema:

> On the screen a strange, slim youth with a long, white face and mad eyes wooed a beautiful lady the width of whose hips gave an archaic but magnificent air to the whole proceeding.
>
> After a while a woman behind them told the world at large that everybody in the film seemed to be *dingo,* and that she did not like films like that and so she was going out.
>
> Mr Horsfield disliked her. He felt that in that bare place and to the accompaniment of that frail music the illusion of art was almost complete. He got a kick out the place for some reason. (44)

This novel's lengthy opening drama of sparring, contractually-connected partners is a "reduplicated" series of events that manages to position Julia as both a dominatrix that never was, and a newly aspiring but failed dominatrix, as it were. Julia, that is, is a woman who in Mackenzie's imagination once had him under her thumb; but she is also a woman he knows to be so weak that the simple act of entering the restaurant will have put her into a state of "collapse." She is a woman whose last ploy to reassert whatever small power she had over Mackenzie takes the form of

her slapping him and declaring that she despises him; yet, she appears to con-
cede an already-anticipated defeat when her slap and insult do not produce the
desired effect. She is a woman who piques the restless Horsfield's interest for
her apparent beauty and show of cruelty; but she is, he realizes upon meeting
her, a woman not of "that sort" at all. She is a woman, furthermore, whose
power otherwise is her ability to render Mackenzie ridiculous; yet Mackenzie
wins the comic duel since his idea of what is absurd ("*dingo*") is that which is
"consecrated" in a thousand popular theaters. (We note, for example, that just
as in the above episode, what frightens Mackenzie when he sits thinking about
Julia is his memory of their initial break, how she caused a scene six months
previously in the very same restaurant: "Julia had wept; she had become hysterical. She had made a scene, sitting in that very restaurant, under the shocked
and disapproving eyes of Monsieur Albert. She had made him look a fool"
[27].) The novel's elaboration of the precise nature of Julia's "after," in sum,
evokes the theater and regime of the masochistic fantasy at the same time they
are lamented as that which has already dissolved.

In attempting to describe the curious mood and nature of this novel,
Mary Lou Emery writes the following:

> Romance has already failed the female protagonist in this novel, and quest
> appears to have died with it. The reader might wonder whether this is
> another "prequel" like *Wide Sargasso Sea,* a novel that somehow ended
> before it began, but in this case ended badly, inconclusively. However, pos-
> sibilities reopen within the narrative for both romance and quest plots,
> possibilities that conclude with the repetition of all that has gone before.
> The novel does not progress, its heroine does not "get on," but neither does
> she decline in the ways that Anna or Marya might be described as declin-
> ing in social and moral status. Rather, readers' expectations for a conven-
> tionally ascending or descending narrative are continually thwarted as the
> novel's structure circles phlegmatically back around itself. (122–3)

This "something else," "somewhere else," or something that has ended
"before it began" is, I suggest, Julia's curious masochistic yearnings in *After
Leaving Mr. Mackenzie:* Julia's slap is the echo of a blow; the restaurant's
"looking-glass" is cloudy and so does not reduplicate satisfyingly or satisfactorily; Horsfield's cinematic fantasy is only "almost" complete—the
masochistic regime in the novel is that which is severely compromised, that
which has always-already crumbled and dissolved.

Part II of *After Leaving Mr. Mackenzie* is the novel's body, its longest portion, with the brief parts I and III functioning as an introduction and a coda to

its action. The most momentous event of Part II, and, indeed, of the novel as a whole, is Julia's mother's death, occurring appropriately as the novel's literal central event halfway through Part II and thus halfway through the novel as a whole. On the one hand, Part II contains the primary evidence tying *After Leaving Mr. Mackenzie* to Conrad's *Almayer's Folly*, links that, as we shall see, take on meaning within the context of the drama of Julia's mother's decline and death. On the other, Part II can be read as a prolongation of the lament and yearning earlier consecrated in the book's preceding chapters.

In Part II, then, Julia is in London, although she is not quite sure why: "'If a taxi hoots before I count to three, I'll go to London. If not, I won't.' / She counted, 'One . . . Two . . . ' slowly. A car shrieked a loud blast" (57). Evidently, since Horsfield is a Londoner and poised to return there the day following his and Julia's encounter, London has impinged itself on Julia's consciousness. Her object, then, becomes to visit her sister, her (long-ailing, quite insensible) mother, Horsfield, an uncle, and a former lover.

Julia's sister (Norah) and mother (Mrs. Griffiths) figure as Julia does in the book's opening. They invoke the masochistic ideal at the same time they are depicted as compromised figures in this regard. The mother, even as she is a type of severe female idol, is an idol in grotesque decline. Norah for her part is positioned as a possible (vigorous) substitute for the (dying) mother, but she seems, finally, unable to mobilize her latent powers. Julia, perpetually the uninvited one during the London interlude, is nevertheless persistent, like a lost masochistic victim seeking to stir some willing torturer (Norah? Mrs. Griffiths?) to life—but she fails to do so. Indeed, the London interlude's ambiguity in combination with its negative resolution contributes to our sense that the book/interlude is somehow about something that could have been, but never, finally, will be: its meeting of women is at times presented as an empowering event for Julia/the sisters, but nothing finally comes of Julia's visit; Horsfield appears all over again and like Mackenzie before him to identify at times as a victim of Julia, but these moments are fleeting and never amount to anything either.

Norah, "a tall, dark girl, strongly built and straight-backed," is maternal and severe, a woman whose defining qualities encompass the particular doubleness of the masochistic ideal: "She had a sweet voice, a voice with a warm and tender quality. This was strange, because her face was cold, as though warmth and tenderness were dead in her" (71); "Her expression was not suppressed or timid, as with so many of her kind. Her face was dark and still, with something fierce underlying the stillness" (74). Norah's "kind," other than this, is, on the one hand, "Middle-class, no money," and, on the other, thwarted (73). Her adult life has been one of self-sacrifice, as it is she who has had to weather the burden of the invalid mother's care over the years. Rhys informs us that she has fulfilled this office scrupulously, but with bitterness, by summoning a passage from *Almayer's Folly:*

> She thought over and over again, 'It isn't fair, it isn't fair.'
> She picked up the book lying on her bed-table—*Almayer's Folly*—and had begun to read:
>
> > The slave had no hope, and knew of no change. She knew of no other sky, no other water, no other forest, no other world, no other life. She had no wish, no hope, no love. . . . The absence of pain and hunger was her happiness, and when she felt unhappy she was tired, more than usual, after the day's labour.
>
> Then she had got up and looked at herself in the glass. She had let her nightgown slip down off her shoulders, and had a look at herself. She was tall and straight and slim and young—well, fairly young. She had taken up a strand of her hair and put her face against it and thought how she liked the smell and the feel of it. She had laughed at herself in the glass and her teeth were white and sound and even. Yes, she had laughed at herself in the glass. Like an idiot.
>
> > Then, in the midst of her laughter she had noticed how pale her lips were; and she had thought: 'My life's like death. It's like being buried alive. It isn't fair, it isn't fair.'

Norah, in the above, is first likened to Taminah of *Almayer's Folly,* one of Conrad's minor female characters. Taminah is a slave of one of the book's many powerful men, who are native Malays, foreign traders, and colonists. However, given the text's preceding physical descriptions of Norah in combination with the description of her immediately following the Taminah passage, Norah recalls also one of Conrad's principal characters, namely Nina Almayer, the half-Malay half-Dutch daughter of the novel's colonial protagonist, Kaspar Almayer: "[Nina's] firm mouth, with the lips slightly parted and disclosing a gleam of white teeth, put a vague suggestion of ferocity into the impatient expression of her features. And yet her dark and perfect eyes had all the tender softness of expression common to Malay women" (14). Given that Nina is both beautiful and triumphant in the novel, and that Norah is in some sense Nina + Taminah, one question put forth here is whether Norah is to be a woman-slave always ("Taminah"), or, perhaps, following her mother's death, a woman who goes on to realize her own ambitions and goals ("Nina"). However, to the extent that a reading of *Almayer's Folly* through

Deleuze (which I present below) suggests that Almayer's "folie" is his masochism, in which the fierce and tender Nina is his masochistic ideal, Rhys's evocation of Taminah and Nina in this characterization of Norah underscores *After Leaving Mr. Mackenzie*'s very ambivalent engagement with fantasy. That is, Norah in the text so often might be, or could be, and also is somehow not, the masochistic ideal. Further, the same can be said of Mrs. Griffiths, a Brazilian Creole whose colonial exoticism underscores and further illuminates Rhys's indebtedness to, and interest in, Conrad's text.

The first physical description of Mrs. Griffiths conveys her severe, exotic beauty, and her terrible decay:

> Julia stared at the bed and saw her mother's body—a huge, shapeless mass under the sheets and blankets—and her mother's face against the white frilled pillow. Dark-skinned, with high-cheekbones and an aquiline nose. Her white hair, which was still long and thick, was combed into two plaits, which lay outside the sheet. One side of her face was dragged downwards. Her eyes were shut. She was breathing noisily, puffing out one corner of her mouth with each breath.
>
> And yet the strange thing was that she was still beautiful, as an animal would be in old age.
>
> Julia said: 'She's so much more beautiful than either of us.' (97–8)

In the text's next passage of description, Mrs. Griffiths' character resonates with Norah's, as she is maternal, but also (punitively) severe:

> Her mother had been the warm center of the world. You loved to watch her brushing her long hair; and when you missed the caresses and the warmth you groped for them. . . . And then her mother—entirely wrapped up in the new baby—had said things like, 'Don't be a cry-baby. You're too old to go on like that. You're a great big girl of six.' And from being the warm center of the world her mother had gradually become a dark, austere, rather plump woman, who, because she was worried, slapped you for no reason that you knew so that there were times when you were afraid of her; other times when you disliked her. (107)

The last passage describing the mother at length emphasizes, again, an austerity, and her creolité:

> [Julia] had been [. . .] remembering the time when she had woven innumerable romances about her mother's childhood in South America,

when she had asked innumerable questions, which her mother had answered inadequately or not at all, for she was an inarticulate woman. Natural, accepting transplantation as a plant might have done. But sometimes you could tell that she was sickening for the sun. Julia remembered her saying: 'This is a cold, gray country. This isn't a country to be really happy in.' Had she then been unhappy? No, Julia did not remember her as an unhappy woman. Austere, unconsciously thwarted perhaps, but not unhappy. (105)

Rhys explicitly indicates once again the informing presence of Conrad's novel in the above, as her description of Mrs. Griffiths' massive transplantation borrows the language Conrad uses to describe *his* principal maternal figure's massive transplantation (Mrs. Almayer's). In *Almayer's Folly,* Nina's mother is a native Malay who was adopted, at age fourteen, by an English trader following a skirmish in which her kin ("Sulu pirates") are decimated (the English trader and his men are the victors). Following her adoption she is sent to a local European convent, an event which Conrad tells us she accepts "calmly, after the manner of people, and even considered it quite natural" (18).

Beyond the way that Norah and Mrs. Griffiths evoke characters in *Almayer's Folly* and (degraded and/or compromised) masochistic ideals, Part II, as I say above, leads us to expect that at any moment Norah will mobilize her latent (Nina-like) powers through the offices of Julia's "pagan tutoring," as it were; but, as I have also said, nothing comes of such moments:

'I'll come to the door with you,' said Norah. She now felt that she did not want to let Julia go. She hated her, but she felt more alive when her sister was with her.

Outside, the sky was clear and pale blue. There was a thin young moon, red-gold.

'Look,' said Julia. 'New moon.'

Norah suddenly began to shiver violently. Julia could see her teeth chattering. She said: 'Till tomorrow, then,' and went in and shut the door. (106)

Or, we expect at moments that Julia will somehow be roused, or perhaps witness the resuscitation of her mother:

'She woke up suddenly. I thought she knew me just for a moment.'

Oh, no, I shouldn't think so,' muttered Norah.

[. . .]

'But I think she did know me,' persisted Julia in a whisper. 'She said something.'

'Oh, did she?'

'Yes, It sounded like "orange-trees." She must have been thinking of when she was in Brazil.' (98–9)

There is also the way in which Rhys lends Julia and Norah's ministrations of Mrs. Griffiths just before and after her death a ritualistic air, as if some sort of female idol were indeed being put to rest (and thus a successor being called for):

> [Norah] had a handkerchief in her hand and every now and then she leant forward and wiped her mother's face with a grave gesture, as if she were accomplishing a rite. (121)

> Norah got up and went and spoke in a low voice to the nurse. She was saying: 'Go and have something to eat—or some tea,' and the nurse was answering: 'No, my dear, no.'
> That again it was as if she were following a ritual, because death and eating were connected. (122)

> Norah bent down, weeping, and kissed her mother's forehead. Then she drew aside and looked at her sister. In her turn Julia bent for the ritual kiss—rather awkwardly. (123)

Yet, as Julia's awkwardness perhaps prefigures, nothing comes of the mother's death; no new intimacy grows between Julia and Norah. Julia arrives to London not knowing why she has, and when she finally leaves, we must conclude that nothing has happened to change her situation. Even her meetings with Horsfield, some of which occupy her last days in London, come to nothing. That is, despite instances where he appears to be quickening to her strange allure once again, "All through the meal Mr Horsfield talked without thinking of what he was saying. He was full of an absurd feeling of expectancy," he and she end up where they did at the end of Part I (145). He ushers her out of his home with a relieved sigh the night before the day she returns to Paris:

> He shut the door and sighed. It was as if he had altogether shut out the thought of Julia. The atmosphere of his house enveloped him—quiet and not without dignity, part of a world of lowered voices, and of passions,

like Japanese dwarf trees, suppressed for many generations. A familiar world. (175)

Once back in Paris (Part III), Julia realizes she must have a job. She composes a proposal for the most degraded of "contracts," projecting herself as the most compromised of "educators," and the novel closes inconclusively, or with, perhaps, the suggestion that Julia is sinking into a definitive alcoholic decline:

> She wrote:
> Jeune dame (36), connaissant anglais, français, allemand, cherche une situation dame de compagnie ou gouvernante. Hautes références. . . . (179)

The long, drawn-out, ceremonial putting to rest of the maternal, austere, idol-like Mrs. Griffiths, in the form of a drama between siblings and mother that intermittently promises, but then does not deliver a resuscitation of the cowed daughters/mother, manages to both evoke and lament a typically gendered masochistic regime. We see, to be sure, in so many of the excerpts above, invocations of prelapsarian worlds: Mrs. Griffiths' life before England when she was a flourishing "plant" not yet "sickening for sun"; a state of nature before a suppression over "many generations"; Julia's world before the birth of her sister. Considered in conjunction with the equally suggestive Part I of the novel, the character types and (negative) resolution of *After Leaving Mr. Mackenzie*'s London interlude (Part II) point to how this novel's very pronounced masochistic contours are in some strange way a sustained masochistic lament. Nonetheless, in terms of recurring (Deleuzian) character types (principal men *and* women figuring as victims; principal women evoking the masochistic ideal) and motifs (contractuality, for example), the novel is otherwise fairly representative of Rhys's particular engagement with the masochistic fantasy. It is also explicitly written *after* Conrad's *Almayer's Folly*, the subject to which I now turn in more detail.

ALMAYER'S FOLLY

> *The deliberations conducted in London have a far-reaching importance, and so the decision issued from the fog-veiled offices of the Borneo Company darkened for Almayer the brilliant sunshine of the Tropics, and added another drop of bitterness to the cup of his disenchantments.*
> —Almayer's Folly

> *When meeting the young chief [Almayer] gave him an absent greeting and passed on, seemingly wishing to avoid him, bent upon forgetting the hated reality of the present by absorbing himself in his work, or else by letting his*

*imagination soar far above the tree-tops into the great white clouds away to
the westward, where the paradise of Europe was awaiting the future Eastern
millionaire.*

—Almayer's Folly

*[Julia's] eyes gave her away. By her eyes and the deep circles under them you
saw that she was a dreamer [. . .].*

—ALMM

Almayer's Folly recounts the final demise of Kaspar Almayer, a Dutch
colonist, who is, from the novel's opening words, a fantasist and dreamer:

"Kaspar! Makan [Lunch]!"
The well-known shrill voice [of his wife] startled Almayer from his
dream of a splendid future into the unpleasant realities of the present
hour. An unpleasant voice too. He had heard it for many years, and
with every year he liked it less. No matter; there would be an end to all
this soon. (3)

After this, Almayer is consistently in the novel a "foolish dreamer (28), a man
"with his head in the clouds" (34)—a man plotting to realize his most cherished
dream of all which is to locate a cache of gold (whose existence is in fact only
rumored). Once having laid claim to this treasure, his plan is finally to dispense
with Mrs. Almayer, whom he has always detested, and to transport himself and
his beloved Nina in glorious wealth and triumphant pomp to Amsterdam (even
though he has never set foot in Amsterdam, having been born in and never left
the Dutch East Indies). Mrs. Almayer is, from start to last (in the narrative present), angry and bitter, having divested herself of her youthful calmness and dig-
nity on her marriage to Almayer. That is, she discerns very quickly that Almayer
is ashamed of having married a Malay and that he did so only for the money her
stepfather promises (but never delivers to) him. Consequently, in revenge over
the years, she has abused her husband in turn, something she finds supremely
easy to do as Almayer is as weak in character as she is strong (e.g. 21; 32). (And
so she is, then, something of a masochistic ideal in the text, even as Nina takes
on this role far more prominently, as we shall see.)

Almayer does not achieve his dream of massive wealth and wife-desertion,
but we are not surprised that he doesn't given what we learn about him in the
novel. Almayer's latest plot is but the last in a succession of grand plots and fantasies, all of which over the course of his life come to nothing. The never-com-
pleted architectural folly he commissions to which the novel's title refers
symbolizes his escapist fantasizing in the book. More specifically, however, the

crumbling of Almayer's last dream in the novel (and his definitive destruction as a man) occurs because, owing to an escalation of hostilities between various trading powers, a partner on whom he is forced to rely in order to secure the gold, must flee. Equally tragically for Almayer, this partner, the highborn Malay Dain Maroola, wins the love of his beloved Nina. This loss of friend, of hope, and, especially, of daughter, instigates Almayer's final and swift decline: he shuts himself up in his broken folly and takes to opium, dying shortly thereafter in a deadly, if perhaps comforting, fog of smoke.

Most pertinent about the novel in terms of its gender and power dynamics, first, are the character of Nina and the nature of Dain and Almayer-the-fantasist's love of her. Conrad's descriptions of Nina lend her a telling combination of ferocity and tenderness, one instance of which I have already cited above in demonstrating how Rhys borrows from Conrad in her characterization of Norah: "Her firm mouth, with the lips slightly parted and disclosing a gleam of white teeth, put a vague suggestion of ferocity into the impatient expression of her features. And yet her dark and perfect eyes had all the tender softness of expression common to Malay women." In general, in relation to her father, Nina is depicted as a character invested with the power either to awe or to thrill him. Her apparent inscrutability and coolness—even coldness—dismay Almayer; yet, when she is kind to him, he melts in ecstasy (e.g. 15; 25; 26; 37). Notably, further, Conrad dwells on Almayer's fending off of suitors: numerous local men, some quite powerful and others less so, come asking for Nina's hand, with Almayer barely able to control feelings of panic in the time it takes to send them packing. When Almayer finally loses Nina, the novel surpasses itself:

> He was convinced that his faith in her had been the foundation of his hopes [. . . .] And now his faith was gone, destroyed by her own hands; destroyed cruelly, treacherously, in the dark [. . .]. In the utter wreck of his affections and of all his feelings, in the chaotic disorder of his thoughts, above the confused sensation of physical pain that wrapped him up in a sting as of a whiplash curling round him from his shoulder down to his feet, one idea remained clear and definite-not to forgive her [. . .]. (151–2)

Indeed, Almayer's peculiar, intense love of and relation to his daughter, of which there is a great deal of evidence in the text, has provoked more than one critic to label it "incestuous" (e.g. Moser 52). As for Dain, he loves Nina in the manner of a child loving its mother or of an abject slave loving his master. A look at Dain and Nina's first encounter is worthwhile, as it captures Nina's type in the novel as well as the nature of the young couple's romance.

Dain has come to conduct business with Almayer, and, according to local custom, Nina and her mother, as women, have been excluded from the proceedings. But, Nina is curious, brushes off her mother's objections, and forces her way into the room where the men are assembled:

> After Mrs. Almayer's retreat from the field of battle, Nina, with a con-temptuous expression, "It's only a trader," had lifted the conquered cur-tain and now stood in full light, framed in the dark background of the passage, her lips slightly parted, her hair in disorder after the exertion, the angry gleam not yet faded out of her glorious and sparkling eyes. She took in at a glance the group of white-clad lancemen standing motionless in the shadow of the far-off end of the verandah, and her gaze rested curiously on the chief [Maroola] of that imposing cortège. He stood, almost facing her, a little on one side, and struck by the beauty of the unexpected apparition had bent low, elevating his joint hands above his head in a sign of respect accorded by Malays only to the great of this earth. (43)

"[D]azzled," Dain has fallen in love at first sight with this commanding, angry apparition, and he is soon prostrating himself at Nina's feet (44). Here is but one typical scene between the two:

> Nina disengaged herself gently [from Dain's embrace] with a low laugh. "You will overturn the boat, Dain," she whispered.
> He looked into her eyes eagerly for a minute and let her go with a sigh, then lying down in the canoe he put his head on her knees, gazing upwards and stretching his arm backwards till his hands met round the girl's waist. (55)

Given the nature of love and romance in this novel, Dain has, not surpris-ingly, like Almayer, provoked comment. Thomas Moser offers the following objection: "Clearly, Dain is supposed to stalwart, courageous, and masculine, and Nina is supposed to be his adoring beloved. But at certain crucial points in the love story, the dashing Malay becomes a timorous milquetoast, his sub-missive Nina *la femme fatale*" (52). Ian Watt has written similarly that, even as "it may be that" such scenes "[reveal] Conrad's unconscious fear that woman's 'surrender' really means man's defeat," it is best to conclude, more cautiously, that the nature of Dain and Nina's romance "subverts [a] convention of romance—the notion that woman is the sublimely passive creature of Victorian convention" (46). Yet, Nina and her mother's estimation of Nina's relation to Dain gives credence to Moser's more perplexed stance: "Her mother was right. The man was her slave" (135–6).

Almayer's Folly, in short, takes place on one level as a story of a fantasist preoccupied with his dream and his worship of an austere, commanding young woman who dominates him, whose life crumbles when this young woman deserts him for another.[6] Yet, pertinently, on another level and much like other of Conrad's colonial novels, *Almayer's Folly* is a highly critical treatment of the complex and volatile power skirmishes that trouble contested, or multiply controlled, colonial territories/trade routes, in this case the Malay Archipelago: Conrad's fictional Sambir is populated and being torn apart by competing English, Dutch, Arabs and Malays, most of whom are pursuing power and profit at any cost. Conrad makes it clear that all save one or two of these men—native Malays, notably—are thoroughly degraded by this destructive pursuit. Thus, the masochism of Conrad's novel is undoubtedly best read as a significant component of the anti-imperial, oppositional energies of the text (even as Conrad proves himself in no way devoid of imperial structures of thought, as numerous critics have established). That is, Almayer, no matter his serious and disturbing failings, is a hero of sorts, a character's whose strange, perverse, masochistic "folie" is a measure of Conrad's sense of the intolerableness of proliferating colonial dispossession. Yet, no matter this sympathetic reading of Almayer's "folie," there is no question that, just as the possibility of Norah's liberation and triumph in *After Leaving Mr. Mackenzie* functions as a counterpoint to Julia's defeat, so Nina's triumph in *Almayer's Folly* vindicates the likes of Taminah and Mrs. Almayer. In choosing a native Malay as husband, in other words, Nina avenges Almayer's racist eschewal of her mother and deals a symbolic blow to all plundering foreign incursionists. Rhys's attraction to and particular use of both Conrad's novel in particular and the masochistic fantasy in general in *After Leaving Mr. Mackenzie* thus points to the presence of an unambiguous colonial subtext. Once, that is, the facts of Mrs. Griffiths' creolité and the invocations of prelapsarian worlds are read as crucial components of the novel's central event of her decline and death, we see how Mrs. Griffiths is the fulcrum of a Conradian intertext, in which her daughter, the masochistic Julia, functions as a inheritor of an intolerable imperial legacy. Unquestionably, in other words, the substance of *After Leaving Mr. Mackenzie*'s colonial subtext corresponds to *Folly*'s anti-imperialism which evokes visions of colonial and or otherwise occupied territories before the defacements of aggressively proliferating commercial enterprises and imperialisms. Rhys thus purposefully cites from Conrad's novel in her text because, precisely, she writes hers with Conrad's very much in mind. This relationship that can be underscored, further, by a consideration of two additional and major intertextual concordances. The first is that Rhys's "phlegmatically" circling plot (Emery) is uncannily reminiscent of *Folly's*. The second is that Rhys's development of Julia's "folie" very explicitly echoes Conrad's of Almayer's.

The novels coincide in terms of plot because neither story progresses so much as it treads water. Conrad's novel hits the same hopeful note over and over again, as Almayer, now down in the dumps (thinking that his dream might not come to be), is, over and over again, given reason to hope. Conrad is able to attenuate these periods of doubt and delay in part because the story is not told sequentially: the present gives way to the past, so that when we return to the present we are with the anxious Almayer once again (who is still hoping that his wild dreams will come to fruition while he monitors this or that situation which will tell him how his chances stand).[7] These attenuating temporal shifts, then, lend poignancy and weight to Almayer's frequent expressions of hope resuscitated, renewed, or justified: "At last! at last! I have been waiting for you [Dain] every day and every night. I had nearly given you up," and so forth (10). Or, there is the plot twist wherein Almayer is led to believe that Dain has been killed—"'Dain dead, all my plans destroyed. This is the end of all hope and of all things'" (96)—but, Dain is not, in fact, dead and so tantalizingly resurrects for the ever-hopeful Almayer once again. Conrad's story of Almayer's tender hope thus conveys his protagonist's captivation by fantasy, his propensity always to scheme, always to dream. Rhys's own circular story, on the other hand, rests on the way in which we are consistently led to believe that something is happening to Julia, but then nothing ever is (as I have discussed above). Thus, even as Conrad's circling story consolidates Almayer's profile as a fantasist and Rhys's emphasizes her novel's peculiar lament, both texts are, prominently, tales of "suspense" and "delay."

But, most striking of all about *After Leaving Mr. Mackenzie* in terms of *Almayer's Folly* is the coincidence of Julia and Almayer, a concordance that also happens to underscore the way Rhys's masochistic commitments are always complexly intertwined with other concerns, especially her feminist project. As any reader of these two novels will immediately discern, both Julia and Almayer are frequently described in terms of bewilderment, bafflement, shock, and so forth. In the case of Almayer, his dreaming and fantasizing threaten at any moment to turn into bewilderment, if and when he is convinced that all is lost to him. In other words, it seems that Almayer the masochist has but one future to look forward to when his world and last hopes crumble: bewilderment promises to become madness. For instance, at the point Almayer is convinced that Dain is dead, he is said to be "bewildered" (76), behaving and thinking as follows:

> Almayer raised his hands to his head and let them fall listlessly by his side in the utter abandonment of despair. Babalatchi, looking at him curiously, was astonished to see him smile. A strange fancy had taken possession of Almayer's brain, distracted by this new misfortune. It seemed to him that for many years he had been falling into a deep precipice. Day after day, month after month, year after year, he had been falling, falling, falling; it was a smooth, round, black thing, and the black walls had been rushing upwards with wearisome rapidity. A great rush, the noise of which he fancied he could hear yet; and now, with an awful shock, he had reached the bottom, and behold! he was alive and whole and Dain was dead with all his bones broken. It struck him as funny. A dead Malay; he had seen many dead Malays without any emotion; and now he felt inclined to weep, but it was over the fate of a white man he knew; a man that fell over a deep precipice and did not die. He seemed somehow to himself to be standing on one side, a little way off, looking at a certain Almayer who was in great trouble. Poor, poor fellow! Why didn't he cut his throat? He wished to encourage him; he was very anxious to see him lying dead over that other corpse. Why does he not die and end this suffering? He groaned aloud unconsciously and started with affright at the sound of his own voice. Was he going mad? Terrified by the thought he turned away and ran towards his house repeating to himself, "I am not going mad; of course not, no, no, no!" He tried to keep a firm hold on the idea. Not mad, not mad. He stumbled as he ran blindly up the steps repeating fast and ever faster those words wherein seemed to lie his salvation. (78)

Then, a bit later in the same day, Almayer is described as follows: "Almayer felt tired now, as if he had come from a long journey" (79); still later in the day: "Almayer lifted his head slowly from the table, and looked at [his visitor] stupidly" (84). Then, Almayer rallies—Dain is not dead. But, then again, he doesn't rally for long because he learns of Dain and Nina's love, of their plans to escape together, and of Dain's decision to withdraw from the project of discovering the tantalizing cache of gold. Conrad ends the novel with Almayer utterly deadened, an opium addict, his "expression" permanently "blank" (154), all

> passion, regret, grief, hope, or anger-all [. . .] gone, erased by the hand of fate, as if after this last stroke everything was over and there was no need for any record. Those few who knew Almayer during the short period of his remaining days were always impressed by the sight of that face that seemed to know nothing of what went on within: like the blank wall of a prison enclosing sin, regret, and pain, and wasted life, in the cold indifference of mortar and stones. (150)

Julia's "bewilderment" in *After Leaving Mr. Mackenzie* predates her second desertion by Mackenzie (12), but it hits especially hard the day she receives the last check from Legros: "She had always suspected that one day they would do something like this. Yet, now that it had happened, she felt bewildered, as a prisoner might feel who has resigned herself to solitary confinement for an indefinite period in a not uncomfortable cell [. . .]." (19). Further, as is the case with Almayer in *Almayer's Folly,* each time she receives a particularly heavy blow, she is bewildered, or stupefied, again. We see this, for example, after the event of her mother's funeral. Initially, in Norah's flat, she appears to suffer a bout of derangement:

> She sat placidly with her knees rather wide apart, and her eyes fixed calm.
> [. . . .]
>   Julia took the hat, looked at it with a surprised expression, then put it on awkwardly. She took out her powder and then returned it to her bag, obviously under the impression that she had used it. (137–8)

When she arrives to her hotel after stopping at Norah's, she is still bewildered:

> Julia turned the key in her door and sat down on the bed with her hands on her knees, staring in front of her with a rather puzzled expression. (142)

Or, if and when she is not bewildered after the funeral, she is peaceful and empty:

As she walked, Julia felt peaceful and purified, as though she were a child. Because she could not imagine a future and time stood still. And, as if she were a child, everything that she saw was of profound interest and had the power to distract and please her. (140)

Julia felt well and rested, not unhappy, but her mind was strangely empty. (157)

If, as *Almayer's Folly* suggests, these characters' bewilderment indicates the definitive impossibility of actualizing their masochistic dreams, then, in keeping with the salient difference between these novels' masochistic contours, Julia is by turns bewildered and roused in *After Leaving Mr. Mackenzie* from the very beginning because her fantasy in the novel is that which always-already has dissolved. Almayer, to the contrary, becomes bewildered only when his fantasy is threatened or when it finally crumbles because his is a story of a masochistic regime destroyed.

These striking textual concordances confirm that Rhys and Conrad's protagonists are masochistic types with Rhys's *After Leaving Mr. Mackenzie* following after Conrad's *Almayer's Folly*. However, as more than one feminist reader of *After Leaving Mr. Mackenzie* has argued, Julia's bafflement is a significant component of the novel's compelling feminist text. One of these readers is Coral Ann Howells, who, despite her reservations about Rhys, fruitfully reads Julia's lonely exile in Paris and London as an expression of women's alienation from themselves, and hence other women, within a masculinist symbolic:

> [. . .] *After Leaving Mr. Mackenzie* is about a woman being locked out from what she desires most. As its title suggests, separation is the main thematic motif—separation from others and a more terrifying separation within the subject herself. This, the most forlorn of all Rhys's novels, is an anxious investigation of the modern condition of exile, from a feminine perspective: how this might be experienced by a woman cast adrift in Paris and London; and the consequences of this exiled condition for a woman's narrative. In this context of anxieties of representation, I would like to take up Deborah Kelly Kloepfer's remark about the way in which representation becomes "both 'baffled'—balked or deflected—and 'baffling'—perplexing, bewildering"—in this novel. Arguably this bafflement experienced by the female protagonist and by other characters in the novel might also be read as Rhys's own self reflexive comment on writing fiction. Julia Martin's skeptical questions about

why a woman bothers to try to tell her story when nobody wants to
hear it are also Rhys's questions about writing that story. (53–4)

As this commentary suggests, Howells's argument is indebted to Kloepfer's
reading of the novel in *The Unspeakable Mother: Forbidden Discourse in Jean
Rhys and H.D.* Kloepfer argues that these authors' works encode a longing
for an authentic female "signifying" subjectivity, as they are substantially
devoted to the expression of the "loss" of "the mother-child dyad," in which
this dyad, following Kristeva, refers to the mother-identified (pre)linguistic
space of the semiotic chora.

Kloepfer is interested in the places in *After Leaving Mr. Mackenzie*
where language breaks down, and she remarks the following, for example,
about Julia's interactions with her mother: "The cadence of Mrs. Griffiths'
bodily rhythms as she lies dying, her whimperings and mumblings, clearly
pull Julia back into a maternal sphere anterior to syntax and signification, a
long-vanished past [. . .]" (56). She goes on to explain that "Rhys encodes
the dead mother both as a trope for textlessness and as an inscription of the
'other side' of language, a space in which women [. . .] might find the
means to signify within and to subvert the symbolic" (58). Kloepfer reads the
scene cited above in which Julia's mother is at first maternal ("Her mother
had been the warm center of the world") and only later severe (slapping her
for "no reason") as follows:

> Rhys evokes here a world of preoedipal images and sensations—
> warmth, hair, caresses, groping, sweetness, mystery—a world that is
> inexplicable because it exists in a presence prior to the need to represent
> its loss. The mother that Rhys describes, however, despite her associa-
> tion as the "centre" of a typically Rhysian maternal geography, has to a
> certain degree already been inauthenticated, long before her imminent
> death: Julia 'had been accustomed for years to the idea that her mother
> was an invalid, paralysed, dead to all intents and purposes.' When we
> read Julia [. . .] as a woman absolutely encased in loss but particularly
> in her absence as a signifying subject in the discourse that engulfs her,
> we can trace her own absence to the absence of the mother, the
> repressed object for which the meaningless signifiers stand in, the
> "invalid" woman who, even when alive, is to all intents and purposes
> dead to the daughter. (53)

Within the context of this particular textual dynamic, as Kloepfer argues,
Julia's bewilderment indicates her failed quest to achieve "signifying" selfhood:

"representation becomes both 'baffled'—balked or deflected—and baffling—perplexing and bewildering," as Julia is "baffled in her project to find the [semiotic/maternal] 'thing'" behind all the talking (59). In this case, further, Julia's mother's severity notwithstanding, the invocations of prelapsarian worlds I point to above encode the text's longing for this (pre)linguistic mother-identified space, and, so, ultimately, as these critics suggest, a longing for a female lexicon and vocabulary. *After Leaving Mr. Mackenzie,* in short, like Rhys's other novels, juggles its various commitments so that each tinctures and informs the other, with Julia's dreamy bewilderment, like other formations in the text, functioning on multiple levels and to various ends.

The masochism to which I point in this chapter is a contributing disposition of Rhys's writing generally (particularly her second and third novels). Such masochism undoubtedly accounts for the moroseness of more than one of the early protagonists (that which is primarily responsible for the overall heavy mood of the corresponding texts), and for much of the protagonists' apparently persisting victimhood, as their "suffering, embarrassment and humiliation" must be exhibited in fine detail for all to see. Undoubtedly this masochism also partially accounts for the sexualized world of Rhys's fiction, the way in which critique occurs so often through, in, and around the duelings of heterosexual couples. Rhys's attachment to traditional female submissions, in sum, is probably less developed than many critics believe, as there is no question that some of what is taken to be evidence of this is attributable to the (Deleuzian) masochism of the texts. Further, in terms of *After Leaving Mr. Mackenzie* in particular and the question of the coloniality of Rhys's "European" novels in general, what the "masochistic concordance" between Conrad and Rhys demonstrates is two things. The first is that *After Leaving Mr. Mackenzie* yields compelling colonial content. The second is that, given Chapter One's reading of *Good Morning, Midnight* as a flaneur novel indebted to Conrad's own flaneur novel, *The Secret Agent,* the question of Rhys's relationship to Conrad's writing is unquestionably a rich avenue for further exploration.

Chapter Four

Reading *Quartet:* "Phobic Nationalisms" and a Postcolonial Ethics

Decolonization is the veritable creation of new men.

—Frantz Fanon

After a couple of early, sympathetic readings, *Quartet* gained its current reputation as Rhys's least compelling novel and now receives cursory attention, at best, in any of the more recent book-length studies of Rhys. To a certain extent, the novel's lowly status is a result of how the criticism on Rhys developed. That is, very quickly after the reprinting of her early works following the publication of *Wide Sargasso Sea,* Rhys's work became the focus of critics whose interest in her work was inspired largely by feminist questions—and the consensus amongst these critics is that Rhys's feminism is insufficiently nuanced prior to her second novel. Indeed, a review of this early criticism conveys the idea that *Quartet,* along with *The Left Bank and Other Stories* (1927), is apprentice work. Of course, this notion no longer holds now that the colonial narratives in *The Left Bank* are being discussed as complex works in the Caribbean oeuvre; still, given this critical history and the fact that Rhys's European texts are scarcely considered in postcolonial discussions, *Quartet* hardly presents itself as a text worthy of a second look.

As for the early, more generous readings, Thomas Staley's is perhaps the most thorough. He reads the story's cynical glimpse into the Parisian expatriate art scene, and its central event—the adulterous affair of protagonist Marya Zelli and Hugh Heidler—as a biting treatment of betrayal, viciousness, and post-war moral distemper. The "themes" of the novel revolve around the "gross and subtle ways in which we hurt each other," he claims, in that all "of the major characters are victims" and all are "motivated by their lusts or needs and driven to a numbness and moral blindness in their hatreds, illusions, and self-pity" (52).[1]

The reading of *Quartet* presented here, like Staley's reading, follows from an analysis of the dynamics of the novel's central event, its love affair. Of equal importance in what follows is the nature of the eponymous quartet of major characters, as well as the particular structure of the novel—or, more precisely, the novel's constituent parts, which are a short opening segment and a body. A plot and character summary is perhaps in order to identify the many particulars pertinent to this chapter's reading: *Quartet*'s foursome is divided up into two couples: the Heidlers—Lois and Hugh (the latter known as "Heidler"); and the Zellis—Marya and Stephan. Marya and the Heidlers are Britons and Stephan is a Pole. (Although since her marriage, Marya is of Polish nationality, too). The novel's short opening segment culminates in Stephan's arrest on charges of fencing, his sentencing to one year in prison and exile from France on his release. Following this prelude, the novel recounts the affair between Marya and Heidler, which begins soon after Marya's move into the Heidler home (at the Heidlers' invitation, once Stephan is imprisoned). The novel ends with Stephan's release and departure for "the Argentine," and with both Stephan and Heidler breaking with Marya.

The highly controlled arrangement of personages suggested by the novel's title accords with Rhys's treatment of the two couples. As I demonstrate in detail below, she characterizes and contrasts them in the following ways: On the one hand, Marya and Stephan are constructed as national/ethnic hybrids, characters most notable for their lack of identity as such; further, they are racialized, feminized, and (under) classed as a unit. On the other hand, the upper crust Heidlers are unambiguously ethnically Anglicized and masculinized as a unit, and they are known for their classism and taxonomical predilections (or, as Marya puts it at one point, their "mania for classification" [118]). The Zellis furthermore are the Heidlers' obverse doubles in another sense. They are their criminalized doubles thanks to the occupations of the two men: Heidler is a legitimate "picture-dealer" and Stephan is a fence of art and other precious artifacts (the latter calls himself, euphemistically, a "*commissionaire d'objets d'art*" [17]). The Zelli couple thus refers to that which is excluded/"criminalized" and to deconstructive energies, and the Heidlers, in clear contrast, to the persistence of distinctions and to that which is legitimate and hegemonic.

That the body of the novel takes place as an affair between Marya and Heidler is intriguing given their distinctly contrasting profiles. That is, it would seem that they should be poison to each other. Yet, in a way, they are, because the affair is an attraction-repulsion one and extremely fraught, with Heidler and Marya the opposites both fervently detesting and desiring each other. Their love is like a madness, and Rhys makes it clear that both the madness and the attraction rests on the fact that they are so different. So, as Marya aptly states of her relationship with Heidler at one point, "But of course it wasn't a love affair," and, evidently, it is not, something else is going on in this highly allegorical novel (117). This something else, I propose, is a modeling of a mechanism of identity related to the novel's treatment of exclusion and indistinguishable from that which has been named abjection, the idea that selfhood is partially constituted through repudiations, so that that which one rejects—or defines oneself against—is a constitutive, if repressed, portion of identity. In other words, in Heidler and Marya's attraction-repulsion relationship—given their contrasting allegorical profiles—Rhys sketches an identitarian dependence on "others," or on the "not-I"; and, further, in their madness, she sketches a "return" of the repressed, the inevitable disintegration of self such a "return" entails. Yet, then again, a theory of identity whose first premise is that exclusionary reflexes are inevitable seems odd, given that the novel, otherwise, sets out to demonstrate the perniciousness of exclusion. Such a demonstration is, indeed, the point of novel's opening: the criminalization and imprisonment of Stephan, Stephan's expulsion from France, and Marya's subsequent destitution all point to the ills to which exclusionary reflexes give rise. Further, given the hybridity of the Zelli couple, it would seem that Rhys might, in fact, be exploring wholly other models of identity in the novel.

The fluid hybridity of the Zelli couple does not indicate an alternative model of identity per se in the novel. Rather, it gestures toward the obvious: the new mixed, less stable, identities of a post-imperial, multi-cultural world, identities other than those which dominated the imagination of Rhys's era and to which the Heidlers (as a unit) most obviously refer. These new identities are, in comparison, more provisional, flexible. Further, in a somewhat related vein, the Zellis' indeterminateness points to the provisional nature of identity as such, provisional not only in the sense that identities can and must be newly conceived, but also in the sense that identity is never that which is fixed but instead requires continuous shoring up (abjection). Last, the Zellis' hybridity set against the scrupulous policing of ethnic and national boundaries the Heidlers represent is a clear critique of (particularly imperial-era) ideologies of national and ethnic purity. Or, to put all this another way, exclusionary reflexes figure in *Quartet* as a core component of any identity, but as a perversely developed component of hegemonic, imperial-era identities, wherein the supposed degeneracy of imperial Europe's others constitutes a primary rationale for the imperialist regime of control. Thus, Rhys's last word in the novel resides in her having chosen to package her allegory about imperial-era exclusion, and identity-as-abjection, as an *amour fou*: in suggesting that one's "others" are to be guarded as jealously as lovers, that one is nothing without them, she gestures towards an ethics of inter-subjective dependence and responsibility—an ethics of self-conscious vigilance whereby one resists, at all times, the lure of ideological villainizations. The novel's body, or love affair, following the opening's mini-allegory of exclusion (Stephan's arrest and containment), is thus a riposte to the opening, Rhys's answer to the problem of (identitarian) exclusion and "phobic nationalisms" (Marciniak 2).

Quartet begins with a lead planted in its opening passage:

> It was about half-past five on an October afternoon when Marya Zelli came out of Cafe Lavenue, which is a dignified and comparatively expensive establishment on the Boulevard de Montparnasse. She had been sitting there for nearly an hour and a half, and during that time had drunk two glasses of black coffee, smoked six caporal cigarettes and read the week's *Candide*. (5)

There is something about Marya here that suggests emptiness. She has, clearly, room enough for vast ingestion: she drinks, smokes, and reads plentifully. Considering that she soon will be typed summarily by the narrator to be "reckless, lazy, a vagabond by nature" (14), it is not surprising to find, as the novel proceeds, that she is a "Candide" of sorts, a rather empty characteriological vessel at the service of authorial "chance," a receptive bodily site over and upon which power flows and encrypts itself. Rhys thus encodes for her readers a salient key to the novel in its first words: it can be read like Voltaire's *Candide* (itself an imperial critique and to which I return in a moment)—its character and plot are highly *schematic*.

The book's title and this opening allusion promise allegory which the immediately subsequent, very neat, opposition and doubling of couples delivers. That is, we learn in the novel's very first pages that Heidler is a "picture-dealer" (6) and Stephan a fence, a concordance of employment that challenges the reader to find a way to describe the fence and the "picture-dealer man" in the same terms. How are they the same man and how does this contribute to our understanding of the significance of the couples' opposition? An obvious start would be to say that what both men do is fulfill the commissions of wealthy collectors. Both are middlemen. Yet, Stephan's unusual difference seems to be the key to understanding the significance of the doubling, as we see only Stephan at work and never Heidler. It is through Stephan's provocative, criminal difference and specificity that we are asked to view Heidler, a specificity, as the following key passage treating Stephan suggests, that has to do with two things: one, Stephan's business is decidedly shady; two, his buyers and connections are interested in "anything" having belonged to historical notables:

> Stephan seemed to do most of his business in cafés. He explained that he acted as intermediary between Frenchmen who wished to sell and foreigners (invariably foreigners) who wished to buy pictures, fur coats, twelfth-century Madonnas, Madame du Barry's prie-Dieu, anything.
>
> Once he had sold a rocking-horse played with by one of Millet's many children, and that had been a very profitable deal indeed. (20)

With this, a most accurate description of Stephan's employment would be to say that he enables theft to occur amongst collectors themselves, as goods stolen from one owner are passed along in shady circumstances to another. And considering the nature of the goods—that they tend to be "anything" having belonged to historical notables or even their relations—what he does, then, or what we must conclude the novel suggests both men do, is enable the competitive amassing of cultural capital. Indeed, Stephan, who reads in *Quartet* much like a stock, two-bit crook operating hopelessly out of his league, is precisely this. What his arrest and exile within the terms of this opposition tells us is that Stephan has been "out-classed," successfully contained, rigorously excluded from trafficking in that which he does not "own."

The events leading up to and including the event of Stephan's imprisonment—events presented in the crucial opening segment of the novel—confirm the novel's scrupulous construction of Stephan/the Zellis as that which is illegitimate/excluded. Specifically, these events are suspended on a series of allusions to (originary French) Enlightenment figures and events that tell us that this problematic of hegemony signifies in the novel beyond the contexts of the present and of class. That is, the entire panoply of imperial-era exclusions is in fact what interests Rhys, as when the ideals of universalism and egalitarianism are invoked, they are so only within the context of polemics concerning class *and* gender *and* race exclusion.

Major Enlightenment allusions are, as I have already noted, to Voltaire and *Candide,* and, as we see in the passage cited just above, to the *arriviste* who was executed for her troubles, Madame du Barry.[2] Then, there is Rhys's choice of the Zellis' lodgings, "Hôtel de l'Univers," a locale whose name refers obviously to the universal from which Stephan is to be summarily ejected (8). Further, what defines Marya's musings about her husband's work in the novel's early pages rests on her consideration of two items in particular, a saber and a necklace, both having belonged, purportedly, to members of the French Bonapartes. The necklace was made for Empress Eugénie, wife of Napoleon III, and the saber is said to have belonged to Napoleon I himself. The saber, moreover and most significantly, is what we are led to believe accounts for Stephan's arrest:

> Sometimes he took her with him to some obscure cafe where he would meet an odd-looking old man or a very smartly-dressed young one. She would sit in the musty-smelling half-light sipping iced beer and listening to long, rapid jabberings: *'La Vierge au coussin vert—Première version—Authentique—Documents—Collier de l'Impératrice Eugénie . . .* '
> 'An amethyst necklace, the stones as big as a calf's eye and set in gold. The pendant pear-shaped, and the size of a pigeon's egg. The necklace is strung on a fine gold chain and set with pearls of an extraordinary purity.' (20; italics and ellipsis in text).

Unlike the painting of the Virgin, the necklace warrants special attention and description in the text, as does the sword and its provenance:

> One evening she had come home to find Napoleon's sabre lying naked and astonishing on her bed by the side of its cedar-wood case.
> (*'Oui, parfaitement,'* said Stephan. *'Napoleon's sabre.'*)
> One of his sabres, she supposed. He must have had several of them, of course. A man like Napoleon. Lots. She walked round to the other side of the bed and stared at it, feeling vaguely uneasy. There was a long description of the treasure on the cedar-wood case.
> 'There are two sheaths, the first of porcelain inlaid with gold, the second gold worked in Oriental fashion. The blade is of the finest Damascus steel and on it is engraved: "In token of submission, respect and esteem to Napoleon Bonaparte, the hero of Aboukir—Mouhrad Bey."'
> (20–1; italics in text).

This "astonishing" and wholly absurd scenario of Napoleon's sword lying unsheathed on Marya's bed is the nexus of the novel's opening Enlightenment travesty and a primal scene of sorts. The founding scandal, clearly, is failed Western revolutionism, and there is a flurry of associations. These are of the revolution's core ideals: Hotel l'Univers; its *philosophes:* Voltaire; its child and hero: Napoleon; its compromises: Empire over Republic; its betrayals: the persistence of classism (Stephan's arrest as a consequence of having fenced the revolutionary's sword); its exclusions: woman and other as conquest (the "submission" of Mouhrad Bey and the scene's connotations of sexual conquest). *Quartet's* opening is thus appropriately rounded off the day Marya visits the "Palais de Justice" to discover what has happened to Stephan: "Shining gates, ascending flights of steps. *Liberté, Egalité, Fraternité* in golden letters; *Tribunal de Police* in black. As it were, a vision of heaven and the Judgment" (29; italics in text). Hoping, all along, that her husband has been mistaken for a "bolshevist," as there are rumors of plots afoot (25, 29), Marya is dismayed to learn that Stephan has been found out for the fence that he is.

Quartet's opening allusive puzzle, in short, invokes the place and era of the birth of true citizen-nations only to mark the era's ideological limits and devolution over time, limits which include colonial meanings as the "submission" of Mouhrad Bey and the sumptuousness of the high imperial artifacts suggest. These details are undoubtedly mustered to remind us of Napoleonic France's desire to out-colonize the erstwhile European competition, and, if we heed the suggestive pride of place which Rhys gives *Candide,* its status as a pointed colonial satire and imperial critique. We see Voltaire's colonial bite in the following South American scene from the Enlightenment novella, in which Candide and his companions encounter a slave:

> As they were approaching the town they saw a Negro lying on the ground, his only garment a pair of short blue trousers which had been half torn away. The poor man's left leg and right hand were missing.
>
> "Good Heavens!" Candide said to him in Dutch. "What are you doing here in such a terrible state?"
>
> "I'm waiting for my master, Mynheer Vanderdendur, the famous merchant," replied the Negro.
>
> "Is it Mynheer Vanderdendur who has treated you so badly?" asked Candide.
>
> "Yes, sir," said the Negro, "it's the custom. We're given a pair of short trousers twice a year as clothing. If while we're working in the sugar mills we get a finger caught under the millstone, they cut off the whole hand; if we try to run away, they cut off a leg. I've been in both of these situations. That's the price of the sugar you eat in Europe. However, when my mother sold me on the Guinea coast for ten patagons [. . .]. (127–9; my translation)

Voltaire's imperial map, a triangle of transatlantic greed and iniquity highlighting Dutch involvement ("Mynheer Vanderdendur"), is suitably re-plotted by Rhys. Whereas Voltaire is interested in the way that Dutch maritime and merchant expertise initially enabled European imperialism in the areas in which France held its interests, Rhys is at pains to point out that the United States and not Europe figures as the locale to which the world's riches are now inexorably drawn. The sword, thus, we learn from Stephan, has gone to "'America'" (21), and the necklace, likewise, will be hung "as quickly as possible" around the neck of a "Mrs Buckell A. Butcher of something-or-other, Pa." (20). Indeed, Rhys's gaudy necklace and rich sword are undoubtedly designed to call to mind *Candide*'s El Dorado, the elusive treasure-topia European greed imagined and which Voltaire conjures with such high absurdity in his book. In Voltaire's golden city most everything is made of precious metals and stones (the latter which litter the streets in piles), from the street pavement, to the clothing, to the drinking vessels. And as for the hapless Candide, he is able finally to escape the cruel jostling of fate, because, naive as he is, he is canny enough to cram his pockets with stones when he heads for home.

As I have said, Marya and Heidler's love affair is a "response" to the novel's opening polemics. However, before turning to an examination of the love affair, a look at the Zellis' counterparts, the Heidlers, as well as further details from the novel's opening, is in order, as this exercise will demonstrate the extent to which Rhys weaves into *Quartet* a sustained opposition between exclusionary/classificatory energies and notions of blending/hybridity. First, then, the Heidlers, the primary, if not the only, representatives of discriminatory energies in *Quartet*. They, as Louis James has put it, "protect themselves by categorising, organising" (24). Their "mania for classification," however, is given expression most consistently by Lois, most significantly in the arena of matters ethnic and national. For example, we are told that Lois

> like[s] explaining, classifying, fitting the inhabitants (that is to say, of course, the Anglo-Saxon inhabitants) into their proper places in the scheme of things. The Beautiful Young Men, the Middle Westerners, the Down-and-Outs, the Freaks who never would do anything, the Freaks who just possibly might. (60)

Lois's close circle, indeed, comprises these aforementioned "Anglo-Saxons":

> Every Thursday Lois gave a party, and Marya felt strangely at a loss during these gatherings where everyone seemed so efficient, so up and doing, so full of That Important Feeling and everything—even sin— was an affair of principle and uplift if you were an American, and of proving conclusively that you belonged to the upper classes, but were nevertheless an anarchist, if you were English. (62)

Further, not surprisingly, the Heidlers' favorite café is LeFranc's: "LeFranc's is a small restaurant half-way up the Boulevard du Montparnasse. It is much frequented by the Anglo-Saxons of the quarter, and by a meagre sprinkling of Scandinavians and Dutch" (10).

What might otherwise in the novel be reasonably taken for Rhys's desire to capture the internationalism and cliques of the post-war Parisian art scene becomes, in light of the Heidlers' "mania," an aspect of the text that exceeds this particular purpose. It functions, more specifically, as an oppressive textual fixing of characters' racial and national specificity. The novel, certainly, is clogged with such attentions. Peripheral characters are consistently ethnically identified, and race and nationality, more often than not, take precedence over proper names. That is, asides and flourishes such as these are typical: Heidler says: "'Lois has got hold of two Czecho-Slovakians and [a] young American—you know—what's his-name?'" (118). Or, there is Marya in this regard, for whom Heidler is always a "German" in a bizarre, horrifying, and fascinating way: "'He looks very German,' she decided. But when they danced together she felt a definite sensation of warmth and pleasure" (63). Or "He wore spectacles. She thought that he looked kinder, older, less German" (66). Or "'Horrible German!' she said absurdly. 'Damned German! [. . .]'" (104). Marya's "'Damned German!'" is absurd because Heidler is not German and because there is, as this "absurdly" indicates, nothing in the text to make us believe that Marya is taken by any popular post-War anti-German sentiment. Rather, her obsessive attention to the Teutonic roots of Heidler's ethnicity is what is absurd, discordant, and a noticeable rupture in the text, so that, in conjunction with all of the other attentions to race, ethnicity and nationality in the novel, we must conclude that each of these things is the occasion for generalized "mania," with the narrator, the Heidlers, and Marya exhibiting the pathology equally.

The references to racial meshing and hybridity in *Quartet* which are set against this programmatic designation of characters by race/nationality (and the characters' own pathologies in this regard) commence with the text's treatment of "bolshevists"—the beings in the novel who represent the revolutionary, inclusive ideal (and who are, in Rhys's degraded world, hounded). Rhys's treatment of a minor character, Mrs. Hautchamp, illuminates the text's work in this regard. Mrs. Hautchamp, the woman who runs Hotel l'Univers, feels sorry for Marya when Stephan is arrested, thinking:

> 'It's a pity all the same,' thought the watching Madame Hautchamp, who noticed that the young woman [Marya] was pale and had a troublesome cough. 'Ah, all these people,' she thought.

Madame Hautchamp meant all of them. All the strange couples that filled her hotel—internationalists who invariably got into trouble sooner or later. She went back into the sitting-room and remarked as much to Monsieur Hautchamp, who was reading the newspaper, and Monsieur Hautchamp shrugged his shoulders; then, with an expression of profound disapproval, he continued his article which, as it happened, began thus:

'Le mélange des races est à la base de l'èvolution humaine vers le type parfait.'

'I don't think,' thought Monsieur Hautchamp—or something to that effect. (32–3)

This connection between scientific anti-racisms and ethnic blending ('Le mélange des races est à la base de l'èvolution humaine vers le type parfait'), and Mrs. Hautchamp the internationalist-sympathizer illuminates, then, the precise systematicity and signification of *Quartet*'s disposition of characters. On the one hand there are the purists, classifiers, and exclusionists, that is, the Heidlers, and on the other there are those who counter them, representing energies precisely opposed to Heidlerian divisiveness. One such character is, then, Mrs. Hautchamp, and another is Stephan, who, as one imprisoned, is a victim of exclusionary energies. Marya, by the novel's end, is unambiguously the most important character set in opposition to the Heidlers; she is their uncontestable, definitive opposite number. In other words, despite her "mania" concerning Heidler's Germanness above, her allegorical status within the novel's schema of oppositions is as absolute "other" and representative "internationalist" *par excellent*. These few words of Heidler late in the novel confirm as much:

'Savage,' he said, watching her, 'Bolshevist! You'll end up in red Russia, that's what will happen to you.'
'I thought that you understand that in me.'
'Oh, theoretically,' answered Heidler. 'theoretically, of course I do.' (114)

Yet, of course, well before this moment so late in the text, Rhys has taken great pains to fashion Marya as the primary signifier of anti-classificatory and anti-exclusionary energies. What most descriptions of Marya convey in the novel, in short, is that Marya confounds classification itself.

Marya is presented in the first pages of the novel as follows:

Marya was a blond girl, not very tall, slender-waisted. Her face was short, high cheek-boned, full-lipped; her long eyes slanted upwards towards the temples and were gentle and oddly remote in expression. Often on the Boulevards St Michel and Montparnasse shabby youths would glide up to her and address her hopefully in unknown and spitting tongues. When they were very shabby she would smile in a distant manner and answer in English:

'I'm very sorry; I don't understand what you are saying.'

She crossed the boulevard and turned down the Rue de Rennes. As she walked along she was thinking: 'This street is very like the Tottenham Court Road—own sister to the Tottenham Court Road.'

The idea depressed her, and to distract herself she stopped to look at a red felt hat in a shop window. Someone behind her said:

'Hello, Madame Zelli, what are you doing in this part of the world?'

Miss Esther de Solla, tall, gaunt, broad-shouldered, stood looking downwards at her with a protective expression. When Marya answered: 'Hello! Nothing. I was feeling melancholy, to tell you the truth,' she proposed:

'Come to my studio for a bit.' (5–6)

In the above, Marya is a prototypical flaneur or window-shopper, but, appropriately, less unencumbered than any male stroller since she is always subject to being accosted by predatory males.[3] Yet, more immediately significant than her feminization in this respect is that she is a friend to these social outcasts who are so beyond the pale as to speak in "unknown and spitting tongues." We are to understand, in other words, that they sense in her some sympathy and likeness, so that she is, first and foremost, another Stephan, the book's most obvious outcast. But, of course, that she is feminized is significant, and she is so not only as a particularly *female* flaneur. She is feminized, as well, because she is small, delicate, and, evidently, gentle-natured. Further confirming this feminization is the way that Esther is masculinized ("tall, gaunt, broad-shouldered [. . .] looking downwards at her with a protective expression"), just as Marya's arch-counterpart, Lois Heidler, consistently is. Lois's first encounter with Marya reads as follows: "'Good evening,' said Mrs Heidler in the voice of a well-educated young male" (10).

Then, beyond her feminization, Marya in the passage above embodies the ideal of (ethnic, national, and racial) hybridity through her naming and physicality. That is, she is apparently only barely physically indigenous and mostly a blend of the racially exotic as a short-of-face, high-cheek-boned, slanting-eyed Briton. Further, married to Stephan, a vagrant Pole whose last name is not obviously Polish, she adopts an identity that, in combination with her own exotic first name and exotic physical characteristics, contributes to our sense that she is designed as a character to connote ethnic, national, and racial blending. Marya as a character, then, is all things foreign, strange, "unknown," something essentially fluid and composite in nature. Together, she and her husband connote a de-nationalizing and de-racializing force and "fence," with Marya thinking of herself, very appropriately, as follows:

> Still, there were moments when she realized that her existence, though delightful, was haphazard. It lacked, as it were, solidity; it lacked the necessary fixed background. A bedroom, balcony and cabinet de toilette in a cheap Montmartre hotel cannot possibly be called a solid background. (8)

"British by birth, Polish by marriage" (35), flaneur, hotel-dweller, and exotic, Marya, again, is not a character or an identity but rather the decomposition of these things as such.[4] She is, then, a characteriological "liminar," as Katarzyna Marciniak would say, a fictional entity functioning in opposition to any "normative idea of the 'I'" or the "self historically conceived within the parameters of ethnic sameness and stable national territory" (2).

Marya's status as the novel's primary signifier of hybridity/impurity is elsewhere emphasized in the text, for example in a section occuring but a few lines after the passage in which she encounters Esther (excerpted above). Marya is by now settled in Esther's studio. She drifts off and stops listening to the painter at the precise moment Esther launches into a classificatory lecture:

> 'English people . . .' continued Miss De Solla in a dogmatic voice.
>
> The drone of the concertina sounded from the courtyard of the studio. The man was really trying to play 'Yes, we have no bananas.' But it was an unrecognizable version, and listening to it gave Marya the same feeling of melancholy pleasure as she had when walking along the shadowed side of one of those narrow streets full of shabby *parfumeries,* second hand bookstalls, cheap hat-shops, bars frequented by gaily-painted ladies and loud-voiced men, midwives' premises . . .
>
> Montparnasse was full of these streets and they were often inordinately long. You could walk for hours. The Rue Vaugirard, for instance. Marya had never yet managed to reach the end of the Rue Vaugirard, which was a very respectable thoroughfare on the whole. But if you went far enough towards Grenelle and then turned down side streets . . .
>
> Only the day before she had discovered, in this way, a most attractive restaurant. There was no *patronne* but the *patron* was beautifully made up. Crimson was where crimson should be, and rose-colour where rose-colour.

He talked with a lisp. The room was full of men in caps who bawled
intimacies at each other; a gramophone played without ceasing; a beautiful white dog under the counter, which everybody called Zaza and
threw bones to, barked madly. (7–8; all italics and ellipses in text)

The ellipses that end the first two of these three passages tie the three
together and in doing so they distinguish them as a unit in the text. Of note
is that Marya's movements emphasize that aspect of her character designed to
connote anti-classificatory and anti-exclusionary meanings. The progression
from paragraph to paragraph entails an obvious carnival logic of place, social
class, and hierarchy. The first paragraph situates Marya in the "shabby" quarters of Paris, where, presumably, the lower classes dwell. Here we find bawdi-
ness, or "the popular," depicted as "gaily painted ladies, loud-voiced men,
and midwives' premises." Then Marya traverses "very respectable" portions
of the city, those pertaining, presumably, to the middle-classes and to "official" culture. Yet, each street Marya treads gradually metamorphoses into its
other, the streets are without end, and Marya's walking is characterized by its
indiscriminateness and unflagging energy. That her indiscriminate walking
leads "in this way" to a scene of carnival festivity and reversal is thus wholly
apt. Deposited, finally, in what she considers to be a most salubrious establishment of gender blending and reversal, Marya ends up in a place where
oppositionality and hierarchy are undone. In fact, if we examine Marya's
other physical movements in *Quartet,* what we realize is that Rhys has constructed her as a destroyer of barriers *par excellent.* This is so because, from
the moment of Stephan's imprisonment on, Marya is depicted as taking reg-
ular bus and train rides to visit him in prison, and his prison is located outside of Paris's city limits. That is, while Stephan is first placed in a jail within
Paris's city limits, after his trial he is moved to a different men's facility outside of Paris. Thus, as the novel alternates between scenes of Marya with the
Heidlers and scenes of Marya visiting Stephan in prison, she is, in effect,
traveling to and fro across an inside and an outside.

Quartet's schematic logic of space considered together with the above
paragraphs' move from "English people," or race and nationality, to matters
of class and territory, to, finally, a consideration of gender oppositionality
and its dissolution points unambiguously to the book's rigorous concordance
with what Peter Stallybrass and Allon White early on in the exploration of
Bakhtin's legacy deemed the imaginary of carnival, or "the four symbolic
domains" of "high/low": "psychic forms, the human body, geographical
space, [and] social order" (3).[5] Such rigor, as these critics observed, is common
in postcolonial texts, in literatures, as they put it, "produced in a colonial or

neo-colonial context where the political difference between the dominant and subordinate culture is particularly charged" (11). This "political difference," of course, manifested in real geographical divisions of space in places like Rhys's homeland, Dominica, in discrete "compartments" and "quarters," as Frantz Fanon has written (37): "It is probably unnecessary to recall the existence of the native quarter and European quarter, of schools for natives and schools for Europeans; in the same way we need not recall apartheid in South Africa" (37).

In turning to Anne McClintock's more recent exploration of imperio-colonial space, we can begin to approach the novel's treatment of exclusion in relation to a problematic we can reasonably term "abjection":

> certain groups are expelled and obliged to inhabit the impossible edges of modernity: the slum, the ghetto, the garret, the brothel, the convent, the colonial bantustan and so on. Abject peoples are those whom industrial imperialism rejects but cannot do without: slaves, prostitutes, the colonized, domestic workers, the insane, the unemployed, and so on. (72)

McClintock's "culturally contextualized psychoanalysis" in *Imperial Leather* parses the abject as follows: there are abject objects (the clitoris, domestic dirt, menstrual blood); abject states (bulimia, the masturbatory imagination, hysteria); abject zones (the Israeli Occupied Territories, prisons, battered women's shelters); socially appointed agents of abjection (soldiers, domestic workers, nurses); socially abjected groups (prostitutes, Palestinians, lesbians); and, finally, there are psychic and political processes of abjection (fetishism, disavowal, the uncanny/ethnic genocide, mass removals, prostitute 'clean ups') (72). McClintock's theory of abjection follows Mary Douglas's work on boundary rituals and Julia Kristeva's seminal writing on the subject, and refers to the process, as I have said, whereby the individual and the social body are haunted by those things which are, or those persons who are, repudiated in order to demarcate the limits of the self and social. Insofar as these repudiated elements mark the boundaries of the self, they are not therefore wholly "other," but rather what McClintock calls an "inner constitutive boundary" of the self and social (71). That which is "repudiated forms the self's inner limit," McClintock states, so that abjection traces "the silhouette of society on the unsteady edges of the self" and "imperil[s] social order with the force of delirium and disintegration" (71).

And, of course, abjection is presupposed in the carnivalesque, corresponding, for example, to Stallybrass and White's point that "[c]ultures 'think themselves' in the most immediate and affective ways through [a hierarchy based on] the combined symbolism" of the four symbolic domains of high and low (3):

A recurrent pattern emerges: the 'top' attempts to reject and eliminate the 'bottom' for reasons of prestige and status, not only to discover that it is in some way frequently dependent upon that low-Other [. . .] but also that the top includes that low symbolically, as a primary eroticized constituent of its own fantasy life. The result is a mobile, conflictual fusion of power, fear, and desire in the construction of subjectivity: a psychological dependence upon precisely those Others which are being rigorously opposed and excluded at the social level. (5)

Thus, for example, Marya's glum musing on arriving at the prison one day: "people are very rum. With all their little arrangements, prisons and drains and things, tucked away where nobody can see" (55). Neatly ensconced in a penal institution outside of Paris's city limits, Stephan has arrived at what McClintock would deem an abject zone and what Stallybrass and White deem the "rock bottom" of symbolic form, "sewers" (3).

While Stephen wallows in prison, becoming progressively physically and mentally abject as the book unfolds, Marya perversely comes into her own when she moves out of the Heidlers' and is situated alone in a small hotel. She has completed her own gradual metamorphosis, alongside Stephan's, once she realizes she has become a "*petite femme*": "It was impossible, when one looked at that bed, not to think of the succession of *petites femmes* who had extended themselves upon it, clad in carefully thought out pink or mauve chemises, full of tact and savoir faire and savoir vivre and all the rest of it" (111).

Marya's seedy hotel is the novel's second "abject zone," a sort of parallel prison: "The Hôtel du Bosphore looked down on Montparnasse train station, where all day a succession of shabby trains, each trailing its long scarf of smoke, clanked slowly backwards and forwards" (110). Marya's view could just as well be of a listless group of inmates pacing below, such as Stephan is likely to view from his own cell. Indeed, Rhys proffers a connection through Heidler: "the staircase and passages of the Hôtel du Bosphore and its fellows [were] pervaded by an extraordinary mixture of smells. Drains, face powder, scent, garlic, drains. Above all, drains, Heidler decided" (127).

The Hôtel du Bosphore is an abject zone in two senses. On the one hand, it is a sewer, the place Marya arrives at when she and Heidler decide between them that she is no more and no less than a *petite femme*. On the other hand, it is a strait of liminality and exchange, an extension of the crossroads it overlooks, one primary locale in and around which Rhys refers to 1) the identitarian instability abjection entails and 2) the ethics that must follow from one's identitarian dependence on "others." In terms of its being an abject zone in

the first sense, Marya's move to the hotel coincides with a solidification of
Heidler's and her character into caricatures of their symbolic profiles.

The fluid Marya is now fixed as a "little woman," as Heidler and she
agree on her place in the scheme of things:

> What mattered was that, despising, almost disliking, love, he was forc-
> ing her to be nothing but the little woman who lived in the Hôtel du
> Bosphore for the express purpose of being made love to. A petite
> femme. It was, of course, part of his mania for classification. But he did
> it with such conviction that she, miserable weakling that she was, found
> herself trying to live up to his idea of her. (118)

Then, the morning after Marya's move to the Hôtel du Bosphore, a new,
super-Heidler emerges:

> He was very different the next morning. A new Heidler, one she had
> never seen before. To begin with, he wore a bowler hat. When they were
> seated in the Restaurant de Versailles she was still thinking uneasily
> about the hat, because it seemed symbolical of a new attitude. He
> looked self-possessed, respectable, yet not without a certain hard rakish-
> ness. There is something impressive, something which touches the
> imagination about the sight of an English bowler hat in the Rue de
> Rennes. . . . (113; ellipsis in text)

Heidler the "German" has become, more narrowly, one British Teuton in
particular, Queen Victoria: "Marya thought: 'He looks exactly like a picture
of Queen Victoria'" (114); "'But he really is like Queen Victoria sometimes,'
thought Marya" (115). Queen Victoria at Restaurant de Versailles? This
points to two major meanings in the novel. First, Heidler as Britain's imperial queen explains his and Lois's effect on the artists they patronize: "Many's
the one we've pulled out of a hole since we've been in Montparnasse, I can
tell you,'" Lois informs Marya, adding, "'And they invariably hate us after-
wards'" (51). So much for the imperial burden. Second, Heidler as Queen
Victoria at this particular point can only mean that at the Hôtel du Bosphore
we will witness Marya's thorough "colonization," as indeed we do:

> He knelt down and stared at her. Her head had dropped backwards over
> the edge of the bed and from that angle her face seemed strange to him:
> the cheek-bones looked higher and more prominent, the nostrils wider,
> the lips thicker. A strange little Kalmuck face.

> He whispered: 'Open your eyes, savage. Open your eyes, savage.' [. . . .]
> She was quivering and abject in his arms, like some unfortunate dog
> abasing itself before its master. (131)

In the above, the bodily topography of Marya displays the forces by which
she and Stephan, her abject counterpart, are successfully subsumed. An over-
determined feminized and racialized body consistently linked to the lower-
classes, prostitutes, and the politically suspect, Marya is the primary site in
Quartet on and through which Rhys inscribes what McClintock refers to as
the "triangulated" or "switchboard analogy" operating between class, gender,
and race degeneracy in "the modern, imperial imagination" (56).

Yet, the loaded scene above depicting the lovers' liminal, "quivering
ontology" (Marciniak) functions as more than the culmination of the book's
treatment of Western imperial-era exclusionism. It is also serves to underscore identity's fragility, the way in which that which is "repudiated forms the
self's inner limit," posing the ever-present threat of "delirium and disintegration." Heidler, to be sure, looks at Marya in the scene above as if looking in a
mirror; she is his shadowy double, his distorted, inverted reflection. Further,
of course, Heidler and Marya's attraction-repulsion dynamic obviously conveys this idea. That is, Marya's love of Hugh flourishes despite her horror of
him, and she weathers the affair more or less consistently disliking him:
"'Very well then, I will tell you. Listen. Heidler thinks he loves me and I love
him. Terribly. I don't like him or trust him. I love him. D'you get me?'"
(92–3). And, developed alongside Heidler's firm symbolic connection to
Lois and hence firm difference from the Zellis, is *his* love of Marya, which is,
like hers, logically inexplicable but impossible to resist: "'I'm dying with love
for you, burnt up with it, tortured with it'" (71). His torture continues:

> 'I'm just as unhappy as you are,' muttered Heidler. His face looked
> white and lined. He began to argue: 'I don't show it as much as you do,
> because I've trained myself not to show things, but I'm so miserable that
> I wish I were dead. You don't help at all, Mado. You make things worse.
> I love you; I can't help it. It's not your fault; it's not my fault. (100)

Heidler and Marya, in other words, both want what they both reject, what
they know is taboo, what they know for their own good they should avoid.
Furthermore, there is the matter of Heidler's psychic liminality, the way in
which Rhys explains his serial affairs with his social inferiors by suggesting
that he inhabits the borderlands of the self and is driven to act out, as Stallybrass and White have it, his "psychological dependence upon precisely those

Others which are being rigorously excluded at the social level" (5). (Heidler's affair with Marya is not his first, and, we understand, it will not be his last.)

Rhys constructs Heidler's liminality by investing him with a constitutional weakness, as Esther de Solla informs: "'I believe they [Heidler and Lois] intend to settle in France for good now—Provence in the winter and Montparnasse for the rest of the year—you know the sort of thing. He's had a kind of nervous breakdown. Of course, people say—'" (9). Heidler's "nervous breakdown" is referred to again, in the context of his otherwise "sturdy" looks, shortly after this (10).

Heidler's psychic fragility is developed in the novel as a form of welling panic he must continuously mask with exterior displays of self-mastery. For example, we are told that his face's characteristic "wooden expression" is always "carefully striven for" (11), so that while his visage is usually "perfectly expressionless" and "carefully arranged," his hands, or something else, give him away: "but when he lit a cigarette his hand trembled" (138). Heidler the "self-possessed" is, in other words, always on the verge of disintegration. He is much like Mackenzie of *After Leaving Mackenzie* in this respect. The only difference between them within this context is that Mackenzie is a somewhat more obviously developed version of Heidler. A look at Mackenzie is instructive, as his profile confirms Rhys's interest in abjection and its implications.

A mostly complacent man who has made his fortune by managing his inheritance well, Mackenzie still occasionally slips up:

> Mr Mackenzie's code, philosophy or habit of mind would have been a complete protection to him had it not been for some kink in his nature—that volume of youthful poems perhaps still influencing him—which morbidly attracted him to strangeness, to recklessness, even unhappiness. He had more than once allowed himself to be drawn into affairs he had regretted bitterly afterwards, though when it came to getting out of these affairs his business instinct came to his help, and he got out undamaged. (24)

Mackenzie's "code" corresponds, loosely, to Heidler's taxonomical convictions, and, as we see, Rhys names Mackenzie's "kink" clearly in this text, namely his keen fascination with "strangeness." She develops clearly, as well, Mackenzie's dependence on that which he otherwise repudiates, as we see here in his attempt to repress any memory of his latest affair (with protagonist Julia Martin):

> A feeling of caution and suspicion which almost amounted to hatred had entirely overcome him. He had definitely suspected her of hoarding

some rather foolish letters which he had written and which she had insisted that she had torn up. One of the letters had begun, 'I would like to put my throat under your feet.' he wriggled when he thought of it. Insanity! Forget it; forget it.

Caution was native to him—and that same afternoon he had placed the whole affair in the capable hands of Maitre Legros [his lawyer]— and he had not seen Julia since. (28)

The panic that overwhelms Mackenzie does not quite tally with things only "rather foolish." Rather, Mackenzie's core terror is his identification with the woman whose dependency comes to repel him, as the scenario of him under the foot of Julia suggests.[6] Thus, not surprisingly, like Heidler, Mackenzie is at pains to perform self-mastery: "Mr Mackenzie answered, with a smile that he had trained not be bashful, that he was quite alone that evening"; "He hid behind a deliberately absent-minded expression" (23); and so on. What characterizes Heidler and Mackenzie, in sum, is the way they inhabit the borderlands of the self.

At the end of *Quartet,* Heidler rejects Marya and, in doing so, he exemplifies the exclusions of hegemonic subjects. Yet, before this return to the status quo, Rhys's treatment of the affair makes clear the very meaningful "dependency" of Heidler and Marya, i.e., her view of identity as that which is at once dependent on and threatened by difference. This point is last underscored in the novel, appropriately, in the scene that records what Marya calls her and Heidler's "*café fine* of rupture." They are seated in a café, and, as Heidler is winding himself up to declare his sudden, new-found hatred of Marya, Marya is trying to remember the name of a man whom she sees sitting at a table near them. He is a "little, yellow, wizened man and his name was—she couldn't remember—something like Monferrat, Monlisson, Mon. . . . something" (148):

She couldn't see [the man's] face clearly. There was a mist around it. . . . Mon. Monvoisin, that was it.

Heidler was saying in a low voice: 'I have a horror of you. When I think of you I feel sick.'

He was large, invulnerable, perfectly respectable. Funny to think that she had lain in his arms and shut her eyes because she dared no longer look into his so terribly and wonderfully close. She began to laugh. After all, what did you do when the man you loved said a thing like that? You laughed, obviously.

She said, still laughing: "So this is the *café fine* of rupture.'

'It is,' said Heidler; 'don't get hysterical about it.'

'Why hysterical?' asked Marya. 'I can laugh if I want to, I suppose. You're funny enough to make anybody laugh sometimes.'

'Of course, laugh. Laugh, but don't cry at the same time.'

'Oh, am I crying?' she said, surprised. She put her hand up to her face.

Monsieur Monvoisin was gazing at her with an expression of avid curiosity. (148–9)

The two supposedly opposed lovers are, finally, neighbors ("voisins"), kin, each other, each other's other half, like laughing is to crying.

Many critics have proposed that Rhys's heterosexual couples made up of a privileged man and a somehow compromised woman encode a connection she draws between colonizer/colonized and male/female power relations. While this is undoubtedly true, *Quartet's* love affair suggests that Rhys's interest in agonistic couplings follows also from her sense that ideologies founded on notions of freedom give rise to structures of oppression, as the affair is a vision of radical *dependence* presupposing an "ethical subject," as Robert Young for example has written,[7] defined in scrupulous "*relation* to the other" (12; emphasis added). Thus, as Young writes in *White Mythologies:* "freedom is maintained by a self-possession which extends itself to anything that threatens its identity. In this structure European philosophy reduplicates Western foreign policy, where democracy at home is maintained through colonial or neocolonial oppression abroad" (14).

Quartet is not about a love affair. Rather, Heidler's psychic liminality and agonistic relation to Marya stage abjection. The couple's affair takes place as a form of eroticized dependency, a conflictual fusion of power and desire, an experience of psychic delirium in which the outline of the novel's socio-political world is sketched on the quivering edges of the lovers' selves. Further, it ends, fittingly, only when Heidler is able to muster some greater "possession" of himself. As such, the affair calls attention to the disavowals of its privileged male character, who, as I have demonstrated, signifies in the text far beyond the context of sex-gender relations. In other words, Heidler is coupled with a profoundly dependent, super-feminized, classed, and racialized female, only so that this woman might be rejected. Yet, in emphasizing so obviously a dynamic of dependence, the novel gestures toward an ethics in which one moves to embrace one's constitutive dependence on strangeness and hence one's responsibility to one's others.

This model of intersubjective ethics which I believe the novel implies is close to one we see developed in Julia Kristeva's writings, following from her own extensive work on abjection. This ethics, put forth in *Women's Time,* is described as a process of "interiorization": a salutary "introduction of [separation's] cutting

edge into the very interior of every identity, whether subjective, sexual, ideological, or so forth" (459). In Kristeva's more recent *Nations without Nationalism,* an extended version of this ethics is presented in the book's attempt to
address the problem of racially exclusionary nationalisms in light of the
French rejection of Algerian and other African immigrants:

> Yes, let us have universality for the rights of man, provided we integrate
> in that universality not only the smug principle according to which "all
> men are brothers" but also that portion of conflict, hatred, violence, and
> destructiveness that for two centuries since the *Declaration* has cease-
> lessly been unloaded upon the realities of wars and fratricidal closeness
> and that the Freudian discovery of the unconscious tells us is a surely
> modifiable but yet constituent portion of the human psyche. (27)

For Kristeva, the constituent portion of the human psyche" at issue is a
"strangeness" within, namely the unconscious (21): "let us know ourselves as
unconscious, altered, other in order better to approach the universal otherness of the strangers that we are—for only strangeness is universal" (21). In a
further elucidation, Amanda Anderson presents Kristeva's ethics in this light:

> Derived from psychoanalysis, Kristeva's cosmopolitanism is defined by
> detachment from provincial identities and by the therapeutic explo-
> ration of strangeness within and outside the self. It serves as the founda-
> tion for an individual ethical practice and as the primary principle
> animating the democratic and fundamentally liberal practice of civic
> and transitional "nations without nationalism." For Kristeva, only
> through the exploration of otherness, and the crucial acknowledgment
> of strangeness within the self, can people begin to "give up hunting for
> the scapegoat outside their group" (51). Psychoanalysis can contribute
> to a renewed universalist project insofar as it teaches the ethically
> enabling truth that "only strangeness is universal" (21). By acknowledg-
> ing this truth, we will cease to consolidate the self over and against a for-
> eign other. (285)

Quartet's carefully opposed couples, its generalized "mania" for **classification**, its carnival imaginary, and Marya's status as an anti-character and tra-
verser of boundaries, all point to how the novel's affair is significant beyond
its treatment of postwar malaise and Marya's helplessness at the hands of
Heidler. There is, clearly, a coherent colonial text in *Quartet* in the form of a
problematization of national, racial, gender, and class identities as they have

been informed by the history of modern imperialism. The busy classifications of the text, set against the fluid Marya and the liminal lovers, gesture at how new selves might be imagined and old selves deconstructed—at how the nation might be conceived of as a "multicultural community that can recognize and respect a multitude of otherness *within* itself" (Marciniak 10; original emphasis). Of related significance is the novel's transvaluation of the concepts of freedom and mastery. The presumption of mastery is exposed as another ideal typical of hierarchical, exclusionary, and exploitative regimes of social and political power in general.

Coda

In presenting colonial readings of Rhys's "European" novels, this study questions the validity and productivity of the longstanding critical practice of distinguishing so rigorously between Caribbean and European texts in Rhys's oeuvre. Further, to the extent that three out of the four novels Rhys wrote during the modernist period have been deemed European, this questioning amounts to a reassessment of Rhys's status as a writer within the modern, demonstrating that, contrary to the general perception, she wrote with colonial questions and problems consistently in mind during this early phase. Indeed, given this new understanding of Rhys, the colonial readings of the "European" novels that have been offered here can only be but possible readings amongst many, so that there is clearly more work to be done in this regard. Moreover, there is further work to be done in terms of tracing the nature of Rhys's relationships to precursor and contemporaneous colonial writers; the Conrad-Rhys connections of this study, especially, make this much clear. Thus, even as Rhys may already be viewed as a writer highly interested in intertextual borrowings and revisions during her modernist period, there remains much to be explored with respect to this early work as it builds on and critiques colonial traditions.

Notes

NOTES TO THE INTRODUCTION

1. My point here is not that postcolonial readings asserting Rhys's competency as a colonial commentator during Modernism do not exist. In fact, many readings of the overtly colonial novel *Voyage in the Dark* (1934)—as well as of the handful of overtly colonial short stories Rhys published early on (1927)—generally establish the fact of Rhys's compelling subtlety in this regard. Nonetheless, the general perception both within and beyond the context of Rhys studies that she is a colonial voice to contend with mainly in the postmodern remains. It does so, in my view, for a number of reasons in addition to the one already cited. One of these other reasons is that the notion that Rhys develops as a colonial thinker over time, coming into her own finally in *Wide Sargasso Sea*, is a commonplace in the criticism—no matter the confusion produced by this notion, as critics who argue this point also often make connections between the earlier and later colonial texts that contradict the terms of the argument. For instance, Judith Raiskin, who is one of the critics who has most brilliantly sounded Rhys's earliest colonial short stories, writes as follows:

    > It is in the context of the analysis of the colonial subject during the 1950s and 1960s that Rhys finds her language and explodes out of a twenty-seven-year publishing silence with most of her "West Indian fiction"—the novel *Wide Sargasso Sea* (1966) and the short stories in *Tigers Are Better Looking* (1968) and *Sleep it Off, Lady* (1976). (107)

    A problem here is that a number of these short stories not only were composed many decades before they were published, as Veronica Marie Gregg most recently has pointed out (1995), but the very strength of Raiskin's readings of the modernist period colonial fictions appears to contradict this version of Rhys's development. That is, can this gloss by Raiskin on *"Again the Antilles"* (1927) really be describing the work of someone still in search of a colonial "language"?

> The story allows us to see Rhys simultaneously asking challenging questions about cultural identification and race, of the sort that Fanon asks later in *Black Skin, White Masks*, and disclosing through the unconscious of the text itself the racial and political ambivalence of the 'settler discourse' and particularly of native white women. (120)

As this second statement suggests, the matter of Rhys having found her voice to Raiskin is not a question of Rhys requiring a decolonization-era education in colonial problems and thought, as it were. Rather, it is a matter of Rhys having finally purged herself of problematic allegiances (certainly not a unanimous opinion in the criticism).

But Raiskin is not the only prominent Rhys critic who presents such a rationale of Rhys's career. Mary Lou Emery has put forth a similar argument, saying that Rhys's writing is a gradually realized colonial project in the way it "place[s] twentieth-century European social and literary values into narrative tension with an emerging Caribbean vision," through "the theater, carnival, masks and masquerade" (7). These Caribbean cultures, she proposes, present "an alternative to European concepts of character and identity" in the form of "dialogue, plural identities, and community" (xii) —but, as she argues, they "emerge fully" only in *Wide Sargasso Sea* (xii).

Much like Raiskin, Emery refers to the "decline" of "a male-dominated colonial system" as being key to Rhys's development as a colonial writer (xii). However, just as Raiskin's readings of Rhys's earliest colonial fictions trouble somewhat her notion of the author's incremental development over time, so Emery's reading of *Voyage* troubles her argument as well. That is, one of her major points about the novel is that its protagonist successfully mobilizes "the laughter of Carnival" so as to "[sustain] her multiplicitous identities" (81)— and, so, in effect, this other, earlier colonial novel by Rhys offers a coherent treatment of an alternative, Caribbean, carnival subjectivity.

This influentially argued idea, in short, most certainly inhibits the amount of attention Rhys's early colonial fictions receive, regardless of the numerous readings proving these fictions no less insightful than *Wide Sargasso Sea*. This notion, further, undoubtedly significantly underwrites the polarization of the overtly colonial ("Caribbean" or "West Indian") fictions, and the rest (the "European" or "Continental" ones): already hesitating to read any colonial fictions written before *Wide Sargasso Sea*, postcolonial readers tend to stop cold at exploring the European fictions. Or, if these fictions are read, there is a predisposition, as it were, to conclude before the fact that any colonial content in them is in no way integral. Thus, since proportionally more of Rhys's modernist fiction is deemed European, this second polarization means, essentially, that Rhys's modernist period fictions are often simply passed over altogether by colonial critics, with the broadest perception of *Wide Sargasso Sea* being that it is a major conceptual departure for Rhys—which of course it is not—not to mention that there is, in fact, little reason to assume without question that the colonial allusions in the so-called European texts are only incidental, or that they can't help us to conceive of Rhys as a colonial writer.

2. My point is that only Rhys's Caribbean texts have received what can reasonably be called colonial readings, not that (general) connections between Rhys's coloniality and elements within these European texts have not been made.
3. Rhys grew up in Dominica and moved to England when she was sixteen.
4. Since discussions of pathology in Rhys mainly have revolved around questions of what it tells us about the psychology of the particular character exhibiting it, or about Rhys herself (in the sense that it may be an autobiographalism), my approach here differs somewhat from the critical norm.
5. In other words, my feeling is that Anna's haunting and ability to haunt refer to more than just repression and point to a periodization along the lines of Edward Said's in *Culture and Imperialism*, in which Modernism is when "Europe, its art, mind, monument, is no longer invulnerable, no able to ignore its ties to its overseas domains" (188).
6. This characterization of Conrad's early fiction in particular as "anti-imperial" in focus is in accordance with Christopher GoGwilt's view of Conrad in his study *The Invention of the West* (1995). (GoGwilt does not, however, suggest that Conrad becomes pro-imperialist later in his career, rather that his preoccupations expand and shift.)

NOTES TO CHAPTER ONE

1. To this statement an earlier passage from the same essay might be added:

> Industrialism and commercialism—wearing high-sounding names in many languages (*Welt-politik* may serve for one instance) picking up coins behind the severe and disdainful figure of science whose giant strides have widened for us the horizon of the universe by some few inches—stand ready, almost eager, to appeal to the sword as soon as the globe of the earth has shrunk beneath our growing numbers by another ell or so. And democracy, which has elected to pin its faith to the supremacy of material interest, will have to fight their battles to the bitter end, on a mere pittance—unless, indeed, some statesman of exceptional ability and overwhelming prestige

succeeds in carrying through an international understanding for
the delimitation of spheres of trade all over the earth, on the model
of the territorial spheres of influence marked in Africa to keep the
competitors for the privilege of improving the nigger (as a buying
machine) from flying prematurely at each other's throats. (107)

2. The novel reports on the consolidation of mass production, advertising, and
   routine department store shopping in urban conglomerations during the
   1930s:

   > Tomorrow I'll go to the Galeries Lafayette, choose a dress, go
   > along to the Printemps, buy gloves, buy scent, buy lipstick, buy
   > things costing fcs. 6.25 and fcs. 19.50, buy anything cheap. Just
   > the sensation of spending, that's the point. I'll look at bracelets
   > studded with artificial jewels, red green and blue, necklaces of
   > imitation pearls, cigarette-cases, jewelled tortoises. . . . And
   > when I have had a couple of drinks I shan't know whether it's
   > yesterday, today or tomorrow. (145)

3. I discuss Sasha's making a spectacle of herself in this chapter with respect to
   automatization and consumerism. In Chapter Three, I discuss this exhibitionism with respect to masochistic "demonstrativeness."
4. In contrast to the thorough achievements of consumerist "conditioning"
   evinced by Sasha's acquaintance, there is also, in the novel, Serge's paintings,
   which thematize this very problem. Sasha has just left Serge's studio: "The pictures [Serge's] walk along with me. The misshapen dwarfs juggle with huge
   coloured balloons, the four-breasted woman is exhibited, the old prostitute
   waits hopelessly outside the urinoir, the young one under the bec de gaz. . . .'"
   (101). Serge's circus scene of jugglers does not commemorate the feats of agile
   acrobats; it is a depiction, rather, of spectacle, of freaks wielding out-sized, garish
   props. The bare-breasted, doubly-breasted female freak refers to every woman
   under consumer capitalism, as a commodified, spectacle femininity intersects
   with already entrenched objectification. These freaks, furthermore, dissolve into
   images of prostitutes, perhaps because to Rhys the "whore," as Buck-Morss has
   put it, is every "wage-laborer under capitalism" ("Flaneur" 121).
5. See n.1.
6. The narrative thread of underground Russian influence in *The Secret Agent*
   is used to refer to the weakening of national integrity in all senses.
7. Rhys makes it clear, however, that *traditional* collectivities have disinte-
   grated, as we see in the following scene:

   > Just about here we [she and her then-husband Enno] waited for a
   > couple of hours to see Anatole France's funeral pass, because, Enno

said, we mustn't let such a great literary figure disappear with paying him the tribute of a last salute.

There we all were, chatting away affably, paying Anatole France
the tribute of a last salute, and most of the people who passed in
the procession were chatting away affably too, looking as if they
were making dates for lunches and dinners, and we were all paying
Anatole France the tribute of a last salute. (17)

While Sasha is remembering here, and remembers, significantly, that
everybody was sociably "making dates for lunches and dinners," nobody,
equally significantly, is paying the author the tribute of a "last salute." Traditional collectivities have thus been put to rest; community under the aegis of
"Empire" clearly must be conceived of anew. Regardless, the street appears here
as the "privileged place of the performance of history," the space of "collision"
between the individual and the "collective" —and this, indeed, is true of most
later, canonical, Anglophone flaneur novels, certainly of *Mrs. Dalloway* and
Ulysses. That is, the commodity-filled public space into which these authors'
flaneur characters are thrown is never simply proof of their homelessness and
(solitary) alienation. Clarissa's sense of being on a rejuvenating "lark" makes
this abundantly clear; or, as Enda Duffy has written of *Ulysses,* for example,
Bloom's pedestrianism is an object lesson on how to give the spreading nets of
capitalist-imperialist interpellation the *slip,* no matter that he is an adman and,
apparently, for the moment, homeless (54).

NOTES TO CHAPTER TWO

1. Much of what Anna remembers or recites is mis-remembered and mis-
quoted, a strategy Veronica Marie Gregg attributes to Rhys's wish to point
to the "fictitiousness / constructed character of the discourse" (123).
Of Rhys's vigorous intertextualism in general—i.e., across her oeuvre, Gregg
writes:

> Rewriting is the major technical and textual strategy in Rhys's
> work. It functions in two ways. First, she writes and rewrites the
> same "facts," using them in different contexts. By so doing, it
> seems to me, she quite literally writes (the) life out of them,
> turning the biographical facts into fictions and the fictions into
> her own provisional and partial "truths." Second, through quo-
> tations, allusions, and other forms of intertextuality, Rhys
> rewrites many of the topoi and texts of European discourse on
> the West Indies. Why? In order to write her self, she has to write
> through the construction of selfhood assigned to her within
> prior and dominant discourses, to read her way through them.

Like Caliban, Rhys recognizes that "his Art is of such pow'r" to shape and name her subjectivity and her place. In rewriting, she is simultaneously critiquing existing readings and producing new ones. (51)

2. See Introduction n.1.
3. See Introduction n.5.
4. This particular notion of the uncanny should be distinguished from Aparajita Sagar's discussion of an uncanny in *Voyage in the Dark:* "By inverting modernist themes of beginnings and *Bildung,* and by presenting the world as uncanny and resistant to the self's sense-making efforts, the novel gives us a subjectivity produced by the discourses of others and not itself the source of meaning and signification" (64).
5. Bhabha addresses the "unhomely" nature of conspiracy in a discussion of Nadine Gordimer's *My Son's Story* (13).
6. Sagar explores instances of Anna's sensuous apprehension of experience in her argument about Rhys's critique of Impressionism.
7. One other interesting thing about this motif is Anna's very specific *relative* contagiousness, that is, the way in which she induces panic in Ethel and Maudie but merely bemuses the nameless man (who comes to Ethel's salon hoping it's a front for a brothel). With Bhabha's point about the significance of rumor and panic in colonial India in mind, this particularity would thus seem to convey a polemic of cross-cultural class affiliation. That is, as Bhabha says, the "iterative action of rumor," its "*circulation* and *contagion,* links it with panic—as one of the *affects* of insurgency" (200; original emphases). Maudie in *Voyage in the Dark* is an under-class character, a chorus girl always hoping for a marriage proposal and in the meantime weathering the company of men who are apt to inform her that "a girl's clothes cost more than the girl inside them" (45). Ethel too is financially straitened, struggling to keep her fledgling business afloat as one disgruntled man after another realizes that she is offering no more than that which she is openly advertising, namely salon services. In other words, what distinguishes Ethel and Maudie from the nameless man is that they are not the beneficiaries of institutional inequalities, rather those apt to be exploited by them. In suggesting that those most exploited in the metropolitan center are those most susceptible to the knowledge that Anna is hosting, Enda Duffy's unhomely idea that the metropolitan imperial subject's "everyday life" was "invaded by a nagging sense of the exploitation and oppression [elsewhere] that made possible its comforts" finds its way into Rhys's text as the notion that those most nagged by Empire's exploitative regime are those who most suffer exploitation themselves (6).
8. As Judith Raisken has observed, "The doubleness of their [Rhys's Creole characters'] identities—as both Caribbean and English while also neither Caribbean nor English—forces them to shift between the two national "realities" (147).

9. Anna's failure to recognize Vincent's hand-writing on the envelop also contributes the interlude's evocation of dreams, as mysterious and/or undecipher-
able script calls to mind (dream) puzzles and the necessity to decode in general.

10. In "Rhys's pieces: Unhomeliness as arbiter of Caribbean creolization," Adlai
H. Murdoch discusses a passage in the novel similar to this memory interlude,
saying that Anna "expresses her discomfiture and sense of exclusion to an
unnamed and unlocalizable interlocuter" in these types of passages, which
tend to be set off from the text in the way they are "couched in internal
monologue" and characterized by an "elliptical style and absence of punctu-
ation" (7). Further, as he says, these passages act

> as a structural and thematic commentary on the main text,
> highlighting through [their] difference from the latter's order
> and linearity the subjective discomfiture of Anna herself. Such
> cases of narrative embedding present a "relation of thematic jux-
> taposition," such as Tzvetan Todorov explains, aimed at placing
> in sharper focus the content and theme of the main narrative.
> This contextual rewriting of tropes and figures already at work
> in the main text fucntion to re-present Anna's disjunctive
> Caribbeanness, and its contrast with patterns of metropolitan
> order and conformity. As a subject, Anna is unalterably divided,
> torn between the recognition of her difference and her inability
> to locate its symbolic center. (8)

11. More than one Rhys critic has pointed to the text's work along these lines
(often in an analysis of the Hester-Uncle Bo interlude, as Hester attributes
what she believes is Anna's promiscuity to a mixed-race heritage and her
Caribbean upbringing).

NOTES TO CHAPTER THREE

1. I discuss Sasha's exhibitionism in two additional contexts in Chapter One:
in terms of commodity display/consumerism and fascism (emotionalism as
an anti-fascism).

2. Deleuze's clear distinction between masochism and sadism gives rise to an
interesting question: are Slave/Master fetish rituals a form of masochism,
sadism, or something entirely different? This question is particularly
intriguing considering the way the historical convergence of S/M culture
and developments in imperial history are an issue in postcolonial studies.
Anne McClintock for example has written: "it is no accident that the historical subculture of S/M emerged in Europe toward the end of the eighteenth
century with the emergence of imperialism in its modern industrial form"
(142). Yet McClintock like others assumes the complementarity of sadism

and masochism ("sadomasochism"), foregoing any distinction between S/M rituals and sadism and masochism:

> For Victorian science, nature was the overlord and guarantor of power. Thus for Krafft-Ebing, S/M enacts the male's "natural" sexual aggression and the female's "natural" sexual passivity: "The sadistic force is developed by the natural shyness and modesty of women toward the aggressive manner of the male . . . the final victory of man affords her intense and refined gratification." (144 and Krafft-Ebing qtd).

3. This chapter does not catalog exhaustively evidence of all of these motifs in Rhys's writing. Some of these motifs, such as mirrors, have been discussed within other contexts, for example the novels' feminism. Others have been remarked less frequently, for example the novels' panegyrics of art, especially of painting, usually within the context of a canvas depicting an image or images of women. (This is to say that, while some—but not all—of the painted images of women in Rhys's narratives have been analyzed, Rhys's paeans to art generally have not been.) My own view is that these motifs resonate on multiple levels in the texts, to feminist ends, masochistic ends, etc.

4. See n.2.

5. Rhys penchant for cold, austere mother figures is quite consistent. Indeed, in Teresa O'Connor's *Jean Rhys: The West Indian Novels* we find an accounting of these recurring figures through *Wide Sargasso Sea*. O'Connor attributes the figures' cruelty and austerity to Rhys having been poorly mothered as a child, a claim Rhys does indeed make in her autobiography although her biographer, Carole Angier, is unable to substantiate it.

6. *Folly*'s epigraph is perhaps worth remarking on at this juncture: "Qui de nous n'a eu sa terre / promise, son jur d'extase et sa fin en exil?—Amiel." This is a misquotation, the original of which reads as follows: "Lequel de nous n'a sa terre promise, son jour d'extase et sa fin dans l'exil?" [Who of us has not had his promised land, his day of ecstasy and his end in exile?]. As Ian Watt has written, the context of this line concerns Swiss philosophy professor Henri-Frédéric Amiel's wistful meditation on the fleeting nature of youthful happiness and the inevitability of adult disillusion. The novel's intriguing epigraph thus suggests how the novel is indeed less an unsympathetic portrait of a foolish man and more an exploration of a man's drive to disavow the unpleasant realities of the day. Of further interest in this regard is Watt's discussion of one of *Folly*'s inspirations, a Malay-Dutch trader Conrad encountered in a Borneo backwater who was, considering his pathetic air and circumstances, very improbably and extravagantly claiming from Conrad's vessel a *riding pony*.

7. Nadine Gordimer discusses this and other matters of structure in her Introduction to the 2002 Modern Library edition of the novel.

NOTES TO CHAPTER FOUR

1. In the feminist criticism, Staley's idea that all of the characters are "victims" recedes, with Marya becoming the focus as the book's principal and female victim. As Coral Ann Howells has said, for instance, "the novel is most interesting and disturbing to a feminist reader in its presentation of a female victim fantasy" (45).
2. Although I do not discuss Stephan's character at any length in this reading, it is perhaps worth noting that Rhys encourages us to connect Stephan and du Barry. That is, she constructs him as a character identifying with and aspiring to the class responsible for his exclusion, until he learns, near the end of the novel, that he has been a dupe in so doing.
3. I address the subject of urban flaneurs in Chapter One, pointing out that the figure's disinterested viewing of goods for sale exemplifies for most critics the commodification of subjectivity. Further, as numerous feminists point out, particular objects of the male flaneur's gaze were women and an early form of female "flanerie"—at least before women were unleashed as urban shoppers—was street-walking (Buck-Morss "Flaneur" 119; Friedberg 420). Here, Marya is both a female object and the object of consumer address.
4. Marya, who Rhys depicts as a committed, even addicted, urban pedestrian, is another literary instance of a flaneur indicating a novel's preoccupation with problems of identity and its reconceptualization (a point I make in Chapter One). The urban crowd and space within which the flaneur mingles is the place where, as Anne McClintock says, "social boundaries [are] permanently on the edge of breakdown" (81). Metropolitan complexity and pedestrianism, in other words, refers in these novels to the flux and mutability of identity constitution itself.
5. Mary Lou Emery, as I have said (Introduction n.1), examines the carnival motifs of theater, masks, and masquerade in Rhys's fiction. Comparing the way these motifs function in *Quartet* to the way they work in *Voyage in the Dark* and *Wide Sargasso Sea,* Emery says that in the latter texts they indicate the protagonist's (varying degrees of) success in overcoming oppression, while in *Quartet* they "measure the degree to which [Marya] has been subjected to the will of others" (112–3). My focus here is on carnival tropes as yet unexplored in the criticism of *Quartet.*
6. Pointing to one of this scenario's additional meanings, I explore its masochistic dimensions in Chapter Three.
7. Young explores such a subject in a discussion of Julia Kristeva's, Helene Cixous,' and Emmanuel Levinas's ethics.

Bibliography

Abel, Elizabeth. *"Women and Schizophrenia: The Fiction of Jean Rhys." Contemporary Literature.* XX, 2 (1979): 155–77.

Adlai, Murdoch H. *"Rhys's Pieces: Unhomeliness as Arbiter of Caribbean Consciousness." Callaloo: A Journal of African-American and African Arts and Letters.* 26:1 (2003 Winter): 252–72.

Adorno, Theodor. *Aesthetic Theory.* Trans. C. Lenhardt. Eds. Gretel Adorno and Rolf Tiedemann. London, Boston, Melbourne and Henley: Routledge & Keegan Paul, 1984.

Anderson, Amanda. *"Cosmopolitanism, Universalism, and the Divided Legacies of Modernity." Cosmopolitics: Thinking and Feeling Beyond the Nation.* Eds. Pheng Cheah and Bruce Robbins. Minneapolis: University of Minnesota Press, 1998.

Angier, Carole. *Jean Rhys.* London: Deutsch, 1990.

Ash, Beth Sharon. Writing In Between: Modernity and Psychosocial Dilemma in the Novels of Joseph Conrad. Houndsmills and London: Macmillan Press Ltd., 1999.

Ashcroft, Bill, G. Griffiths, and H. Tiffin. *The Empire Writes Back: Theory and Practice in Post-Colonial Literatures.* London: Routledge, 1989.

Bakhtin, Mikhail. *Rabelais and His World.* Trans. Hélène Iswolsky. Bloomington: Indiana University Press, 1984.

Barkan, Elazar and Ronald Bush. *"Introduction." Prehistories of the Future: The Primitivist Project and the Culture of Modernism.* Stanford: Stanford University Press, 1995.

Benjamin, Walter. *Illuminations.* Trans. Harry Zohn. New York: Schocken Books, 1968.

Bhabha, Homi K. *The Location of Culture.* London: Routledge, 1994.

Bowlby, Rachel. *"Walking, women and writing: Virginia Woolf as flâneuse." New Feminist Discourses: Critical Essays on Theories and Texts.* Isobel Armstrong, ed. London: Routledge, 1992.

———. *Just Looking: Consumer Culture in Dreiser, Gissing and Zola.* New York and London: Methuen, 1985.

Buck-Morss, Susan. *The Dialectics of Seeing: Walter Benjamin and the Arcades Project.* Cambridge, Massachusetts and London, England: The MIT Press, 1989.

———. *"The Flaneur, the Sandwichman and the Whore: The Politics of Loitering."* *New German Critique.* 39 (1986): 99–140.

Chancer, Lynn S. *Sadomasochism in Everyday Life: the dynamics of power and powerlessness.* New Brunswick: Rutgers University Press, 1992.

Chow, Rey. *"Postmodern Automatons."* *Feminists Theorize the Political.* Eds. Judith Butler and Joan W. Scott. New York and London: Routledge, 1992.

Clifford, James. *The Predicament of Culture: Twentieth-Century Ethnography, Literature, and Art.* Cambridge, Massachusetts and London, England: Harvard University Press, 1988.

Cohen, Scott. *"The Empire From the Street: Virginia Woolf, Wembley, and Imperial Monuments."* *Modern Fiction Studies.* 50:1 (Spring 2004): 85–110.

Conrad, Joseph. *Almayer's Folly: A Story of an Eastern River.* New York: The Modern Library, 2002.

———. *"Autocracy and War."* *Notes on Life and Letters. The Collected Works of Joseph Conrad. Vol. XIX.* London: Routledge/Thoemmes Press, 1995.

———. *The Secret Agent.* Ware, Hertfordshire: Wordsworth Editions Limited, 1993.

Deleuze, Gilles. *Masochism.* (*Coldness and Cruelty:* Gilles Deleuze; *Venus in Furs:* Leopold von Sacher Masoch.) New York: Zone Books, 1991.

Duffy, Enda. *The Subaltern Ulysses.* Minneapolis: University of Minnesota Press, 1994.

Erdinast-Vulcan, Daphna. *"'Sudden Holes in Space and Time': Conrad's Anarchist Aesthetics in The Secret Agent."* *Conrad's Cities: Essays for Hans van Marle.* Ed. Gene Moore. Amsterdam: Rodolphi, 1992: 207–21.

Emery, Mary Lou. *Jean Rhys at "World's End": Novels of Colonial and Sexual Exile.* Austin: University of Texas Press, 1990.

Fanon, Frantz. *The Wretched of the Earth.* Trans. Constance Farrington. New York: Grove Press, 1963.

Freud, Sigmund. *"The Economic Problem of Masochism."* *Collected Papers.* Vol. II. Authorized translation under the supervision of Joan Riviere. London: The Hogarth Press, 1950.

———. *"Femininity."* *New Introductory Lectures.* Trans. and Ed. James Strachey. New York: W. W. Norton Co. Inc., 1965.

———. *The Interpretation of Dreams.* Trans. Dr. A. A. Brill. New York: The Modern Library, 1994.

———. *"The 'Uncanny.'"* *The Standard Edition of the Complete Psychological Works of Sigmund Freud. Vol. XVII* (1917–1919). Trans. and Ed. James Strachey. London: The Hogarth Press, 1955.

Friedberg, Anne. *"Les Flâneurs du Mal(l): Cinema and the Postmodern Condition."* *PMLA.* 106.3 (May 1991): 419–431.

Gardiner, Judith Keegan. *"Good Morning, Midnight: Goodnight, Modernism."* *Boundary 2.* 11:1–2 (1982–1983 Fall-Winter): 233–251.

Glissant, Édouard. *Poetics of relation.* Trans. Betsy Wing. Ann Arbor: University of Michigan Press, 1997.

Goebel, Rolf J. *"Benjamin's Flaneur in Japan: Urban Modernity and Conceptual Relocation."* The German Quarterly. 71.4 (Fall 1998): 377–391.

GoGwilt, Christopher. *The Invention of the West: Joseph Conrad and the Double-Mapping of Europe and Empire.* Stanford: Stanford University Press, 1995.

Gordimer, Nadine. *"Introduction."* Almayer's Folly: A Story of an Eastern River. New York: The Modern Library, 2002.

Gregg, Veronica Marie. *Jean Rhys's Historical Imagination: Reading and Writing the Creole.* Chapel Hill: University of North Carolina Press, 1995.

Hinsley, Curtis M. *"Strolling through the Colonies."* Walter Benjamin and the Demands of History. Michael P. Steinberg, ed. Ithaca: Cornell University Press, 1996.

Hite, Molly. *The Other Side of the Story: Structures and Strategies of Contemporary Feminist Narrative.* Ithaca: Cornell University Press, 1989.

Holden, Kate. *Formations of Discipline and Manliness: culture, politics and 1930s women's writing."* Journal of Gender Studies. 8.2 (1999): 141–157.

Howells, Coral Ann. *Jean Rhys.* New York: St. Martin's Press, 1991.

James, Louis. *Jean Rhys.* London: Longman, 1978.

Jameson, Fredric. *Postmodernism, or, The Cultural Logic of Late Capitalism.* Durham: Duke University Press, 1991.

Keohane, Kieran. *"The Revitalization of the City and the Demise of Joyce's Utopian Modern Subject."* Theory, Culture & Society. 19:3 (2002 June): 29–49.

Kloepfer, Deborah Kelly. *The Unspeakable Mother: Forbidden Discourse in Jean Rhys and H.D.* Ithaca and London: Cornell University Press, 1989.

Kristeva, Julia. *Nations Without Nationalism.* Trans. Leon S. Roudiez. New York: Columbia University Press, 1993.

———. *Powers of Horror: an essay on abjection.* Trans. Leon S. Roudiez. New York: Columbia University Press, 1982.

———. *"Women's Time."* Feminisms: an anthology of literary theory and criticism. Eds. Robyn R. Warhol and Diane Price Herndl. New Brunswick: Rutgers University Press, 1996.

Liston, Mairi. *"'Le Spectacle de la rue': Edmond de Goncourt and the Siege of Paris."* Nineteenth-Century French Studies. Fall-Winter 2003 v32 i1–2: 58–70.

Lyotard, Jean-Francois. *The Postmodern Condition: A Report on Knowledge.* Trans. Geoff Bennington and Brian Massumi. Minneapolis: University of Minnesota Press, 1984.

Marciniak, Katarzyna. *"Transnational Anatomies of Exile and Abjection in Milcho Manchevski's Before the Rain (1994)."* Cinema Journal. 43:1 (2003 Fall): 63–84.

McClintock, Anne. *Imperial Leather: Race, Gender, and Sexuality in the Colonial Contest.* New York: Routledge, 1995.

Morrison, Toni. *"Memory, Creation, Writing."* Thought 59 (1984): 385–90.

———. *"Unspeakable Things Unspoken: the Afro-American Presence in American Literature."* Michigan Quarterly Review. 28 (1989): 1–34.

Moser, Thomas. *Joseph Conrad: achievement and decline.* Cambridge: Harvard University Press, 1957.

Naipaul, V.S. *"Without a Dog's Chance." Review of Rhys's After Leaving Mr. Mackenzie.* New York Review of Books. 18 May 1972: 29–31.

North, Michael. *"Modernism's African Mask: The Stein and Picasso Collaboration." Prehistories of the Future: The Primitivist Project and the Culture of Modernism.* Eds. Elazar Barkan and Ronald Bush. Stanford: Stanford University Press, 1995.

O'Connor, Teresa. *Jean Rhys: The West Indian Novels.* New York and London: New York University Press, 1986.

Parry J. H. and P. M. Sherlock. *A Short History of the West Indies.* New York: St. Martin's Press, 1968.

Du Plessis, Rachel Blau. *Writing Beyond the Ending: Narrative Strategies of Twentieth-Century Women Writers.* Bloomington: Indiana University Press, 1985.

Raiskin, Judith. *Snow on the Cane Fields: Women's Writing and Creole Subjectivity.* Minneapolis: University of Minnesota Press, 1996.

Ray, Martin. *"The Landscape of The Secret Agent." Conrad's Cities: Essays for Hans van Marle.* Ed. Gene Moore. Amsterdam: Rodolphi, 1992: 197–206.

Reik, Theodor. *Masochism in Modern Man.* Trans. Margaret H. Beigel and Gertrud M. Kurth. New York, Toronto: Farrar & Rinehart, 1941.

Rhys, Jean. *After Leaving Mr. Mackenzie.* London and New York: W.W. Norton & Co., 1997.

———. *Good Morning, Midnight.* London and New York: W.W. Norton & Co., 1986.

———. *The Left Bank & Other Stories.* Freeport, New York: Books for Libraries Press, 1970.

———. *Quartet.* London and New York: W.W. Norton & Co., 1997.

———. *Voyage in the Dark.* New York and London: W.W. Norton & Co., 1982.

———. *Wide Sargasso Sea.* London and New York: W.W. Norton & Co., 1982.

Ross, Stephen. *Conrad and Empire.* Columbia and London: University of Missouri Press, 2004.

Sagar, Aparajita. *Forays into the Attic: The Postcolonial fiction of Jean Rhys and J.M. Coetzee.* Ph.D. dissertation, University of Illinois at Urbana-Champaign, 1991.

Said, Edward. *Culture and Imperialism.* New York: Knopf, 1993.

Savory, Elaine. *"Ex/Isle: Separation, Memory and Desire in Caribbean Women's Writing." MaComère: A Journal of the Association of Caribbean Women Writers and Scholars.* 1(1998): 170–178.

———. *Jean Rhys.* Cambridge, U.K., New York: Cambridge University Press, 1998.

Shields, Rob. *"Fancy Footwork: Walter Benjamin's notes on flânerie." The Flâneur.* Ed. Keith Tester. London and New York: Routledge, 1994.

Smilowitz, Erika. *"Child-like Women and Paternal Men: Colonialism in Jean Rhys's Fiction." Ariel: A Review of International Literature.* (special edition: Commonwealth Women Writers) 17, No. 4, (October 1986): 93–103.

Staley, Thomas F. *Jean Rhys: A Critical Study.* London: Macmillan, 1979.

Stallybrass, Peter and Allon White. *The Politics and Poetics of Transgression.* Ithaca: Cornell University Press, 1986.

Streip, Katherine. *"'Just a Cérébrale': Jean Rhys, Women's Humor, and Ressentiment."* *Representations.* 45 (Winter 1994): 117–144.

Tiffen, Helen. *"Mirror and Mask: Colonial Motifs in the Novels of Jean Rhys."* *World Literature Written in English.* 17 (1978): 328–41.

Voltaire. *Candide ou L'Optimisme.* Paris: Librairie Marcel Didier, 1957.

Watt, Ian. *Conrad in the nineteenth century.* Berkeley: University of California Press, 1979.

———. *Essays on Conrad.* Cambridge, U.K., New York: Cambridge University Press, 2000.

Williams, Eric. *From Columbus to Castro: The History of Caribbean 1492–1969.* New York: Vintage, 1984.

Young, Robert. *White Mythologies: writing history and the West.* London and New York: Routledge, 1990.

Index